The Generational Imperative

UNDERSTANDING GENERATIONAL DIFFERENCES

IN THE WORKPLACE, MARKETPLACE,

AND LIVING ROOM

Chuck Underwood

ISBN-13: 978-0-9795745-0-4
Library of Congress Control Number: 2007905692
BookSurge
North Charleston, South Carolina

Visit **www.amazon.com**
or **www.booksurge.com**
to purchase additional copies.

DEDICATION

See if you agree with this:

The most important nanosecond in each of our lives is also the nanosecond over which we have *absolutely no control.* An instant when we're at the complete mercy of "luck": either very good luck or very bad luck, or somewhere in between.

It's the moment we're born.

In that instant, we have no control over the year in which we will arrive on the planet and, thus, no control over the years that will become our all-important *formative years,* when the unique times and teachings of the era will mold us *for life.*

No control over the country, state, and town in which we are born. No control over the parents to whom we are born. And no control over the genetic code those parents will pass on to us; a code that will go a long way in determining our chances in life for good – or bad – mental health, emotional health, and physical health.

Well…

This book's dedication is offered by a guy who, no matter how difficult his career and personal life passages have occasionally been, nonetheless gives humble thanks every single day that, during the most important nanosecond in *his* life, he couldn't have gotten luckier.

Lucky enough to be born in the United States, at a time when only one out of roughly every twenty births in the world occurred in the United States. I was that one of twenty. If you were born in America, you were too.

Born and raised in the vital and diverse state of Ohio. In the safe and nurturing Mayberry-like cocoon of hometown Miamisburg. In a year that meant my formative years would coincide with one of the most joyous, optimistic, and enlightening periods in American history.

And most fortunately of all, born to Robert C. and Geraldine L. Underwood. "Pork and Gerry." Whose selfless and passionate dedication to their parenting of sister Marcy and me is as close to God as I ever expect to get while on earth. Like Norman Rockwell's paintings, Mom and Dad have always imbued their two kids with their own sense of *love* and *hope*, as well as their strength, intelligence, integrity, idealism and aspirations. They also passed down to us their own G.I. Generation's can-do values of empowerment and engagement, along with an unshakable humanism: a belief that all of us, if presented with the facts, will consistently make the right decisions that lead to a better world.

Mom and Dad, because of you, I will – no matter what – always feel like the luckiest kid on the planet. Words like worship, revere, and cherish are inadequate. You are my life. I love you beyond my ability to put in words.

And, sis…

Indescribable thanks for your support during all those uncertain years, when a few of us generational pioneers were banging our fists on the doors of corporate America, trying to convince them to embrace what we were creating. Without your no-questions-asked "being there" in so many ways, I couldn't have outlasted the passage through that long tunnel. We truly didn't know if generational study would ever reach daylight. But now, at long last, *oh my*. My relief, satisfaction, and joy are yours to share.

THE STORY BEHIND THE STORY
AND ACKNOWLEDGEMENTS

In the 1980s, my sports play-by-play career was advancing nicely, calling major college games for the Big Ten Conference and then ESPN, and then hosting a nationally syndicated, sports-entertainment show from Hollywood called *RollerGames*. But to my own surprise, I was also growing bored with the "sameness" of sport and sportscasting. From my career, I was beginning to realize I wanted *more*.

As good luck would have it:

At *Cooker Bar & Grille* in Columbus, Ohio, one evening in the mid-1980s, ten of us filled a big long booth for dinner. We had all become new acquaintances at a recent party thrown by a bunch of unattached, high-achieving career women who worked obsessively at the corporate headquarters of *The Limited*. For a decade, these workaholic ladies had seldom taken time to socialize but finally declared *enough*! They threw a Wednesday evening poolside party at a condo complex, telling each other to invite any guy friends they knew on the theory that "one woman's trash might be another woman's treasure." A buddy of mine overheard their party-planning discussion at a T.G.I. Friday's restaurant and phoned me on their behalf to invite me, adding, "They'll probably even welcome a guy *like you.*" Hmmm. I went to the party and promptly befriended a gaggle of dynamic women, as well as a couple of the guys who had come.

Soon after the party came that night at *Cooker* with the ten of us. The restaurant booth seemed too long for a group conversation, so we splintered into mini-chats. I found myself sitting across the booth from one of the guys who had attended the party, a local architect who is about fifteen years my senior. I don't even remember what we were discussing, but at one point I said to him, "You know, Pat, I'll bet you and I feel differently about this topic because *you and I came of age during different times.*"

As he and I explored that thought, the other talk around the booth gradually came to a halt, as the other members of the group first listened and then wanted to weigh in on our discussion. When they did, the conversation *ignited.*

What followed were several hours of explosive and riveting discussion, all of it coming from a point of view none of us had ever considered and knew a thing about.

MY generation! YOUR generation! My generation believes THIS! Well, mine believes THAT! Well, I think your generation is wrong! Well, I think we're right!

At the end of the evening, I left the restaurant scratching my head and asking myself, *What the heck just happened in there?*

What had happened… was generational dynamics.

Because I was already preparing to leave sportscasting in order to try my hand at creating and producing original TV programs, my first thought was, *Could generational differences be the premise for a Phil Donahue-like daytime talk show?*

The Internet hadn't yet arrived, so I searched the bookstores and libraries for any kind of research or literature on "generations." Nothing. So for the next *ten years,* I was forced to form my own ideas about generational dynamics in solitude, while I produced a few modest TV shows and hosted a nationally syndicated sports-entertainment show from Los Angeles called *RollerGames.*

I spent a good chunk of the '90s trying to explain my idea for a generations-based talk show to TV executives in New York and Los Angeles. I even enjoyed the consulting assistance of Mr. Daytime Talk Show Executive himself, Dick Thrall, the revered and longtime chairman of the Daytime Emmy Awards Selection Committee and the principled, visionary man who had helped to guide the astounding syndication success of *Donahue,* which all these years later remains perhaps the most important non-news program in television history.

But I got nowhere with the TV gurus. A typical response was the one I heard from the VP of Program Development at Columbia Pictures when we met on the studio lot in Los Angeles: "It's the '90s. Right now, the (sleazy) daytime talk show concepts are getting good ratings. We're not especially proud of it, but viewers are watching. In fact, to get away from the talk genre, we're going to try to syndicate game shows this coming season. We don't know if they'll work, but we're moving away from 'talk.' So, no, we won't give you money to produce a pilot for another talk show; it's not our new direction. But if you find a way to get it produced on your own, we'd like to see the tape because we'll welcome a clean talk show that can deliver ratings." Similar rejections from all of the other major syndication companies in L.A. and New York. Dead end.

Then, in the late '90s, rummaging through a half-price bookstore one Sunday, I stumbled upon a paperback book entitled *Generations: The History of America's Future, 1584 to 2069.* I practically lunged at the bookshelf. I read it and tracked down the coauthors, Bill Strauss and Neil Howe, both living with their families in suburban Washington, D.C. We exchanged information. We were, I think, kind of relieved to connect with each other. *Hey, we're not alone in our pursuit of this 'generations thing'!* As we got acquainted, we learned the lightbulb above our heads had lit up at about the same time a decade earlier. *Generations!*

Finally, in 2001, some fifteen long years after that accidental conversation at *Cooker,* I caught a break. A health care corporation, whose marketing VP had remembered me from my old play-by-play days, generously gave me a few thousand underwriting dollars to produce a one-hour TV talk show special that would air on only a few public TV stations around Ohio. It was a "test" show.

Despite the underwriting, it would still be a very low-budget production. So I knew the show would be mediocre at best, and probably not even that.

I flew Strauss and Howe from Washington to the public TV station in Dayton, Ohio, where we taped two and a half hours in order to get an edited-down one-hour show. I was right. The production itself was ugly and un-polished. But what I learned from our featured onstage guests and from our studio audience – all of whom were energetic and insightful and fabulous – would become the light at the end of the tunnel. Generational dynamics fascinated and engaged them. And stirred passionate and intimate revelations and debate. They wanted to talk about their own generation. And about their kids' generations. And their parents' generations.

They wanted to talk.

Eureka.

I still didn't know exactly how to convert this ragged TV special into a regular show on national television. But six months later, fate spun me in a different direction.

In early 2002, I got a phone call out of the blue from a speakers' bureau in Washington, D.C., asking if I would come to the nation's capital and conduct a workshop about Generational Marketing Strategy at the prestigious National Summit on Retirement Savings, a congressionally mandated conference for three hundred of the nation's elite senior-level executives in banking, finance, insurance, and investing. "Sure," I answered.

The speakers' bureau rep said, "Good, glad to hear you're available; we'll call you back in a few hours with the details, but you'll be speaking right before Federal Reserve Chairman Alan Greenspan and President Bush." *What?* And that's what happened.

As it turns out, my talk show guests Strauss and Howe

had recommended me for the presentation, so I phoned them immediately after taking the call from the speakers' bureau. I thanked them for the referral, but also expressed concern that, since I had never presented this topic as a *business* strategy, I might damage their reputation with a bad speech. Their reply scared and thrilled me. "You have to understand: we and you are at the leading edge of this field of study. These executives have never heard anything about generational dynamics. Accept the assignment, give it your best research, and just watch what happens." And so I did.

Sure enough, the executives who attended the "Saver Summit" had no idea what to expect from this curious conference theme of *generational marketing*. As one female attendee from St. Louis said when the three-day event had ended, "When I heard the topic was going to be *generations*, I flashed back to my 'singles' days in the '70s, when the guys who approached me in the bar would ask, 'What's your sign?' I thought I was going to spend three days at this conference with people asking me, 'What's your generation?'"

Another attendee, a distinguished-looking president of a Midwest bank, convinced me that Strauss and Howe, and now I and only a very few others, were on to something special. At the end of the second day of this conference, the bank president felt compelled to interrupt the conversation in our room and say to his fellow attendees, "I just want to say that I came to the first Saver Summit four years ago, and I learned so little that I almost didn't come to this one. *But this generations stuff is the best information I've ever heard.*" Virtually every head in the room nodded in enthusiastic agreement.

Sure enough, Saver Summit attendees came up after-ward and launched my career in generational consult-ing. "Consult our company." "Speak at our national con-vention." "Send me your information."

One gentleman looked at me very intensely, and pro-phetically said, "I hope you know what you're on to."

So I shifted my thinking from a generational television show concept to generational business consulting.

A few months after the Saver Summit, Mindy Good, a cherished friend who now handles public information for the Washington, D.C. Department of Child and Family Services and who knew about my work, introduced me to the program chairwoman of the Cincinnati Advertising Club. Long story short: I presented a luncheon key-note address on Generational Advertising Strategy at a monthly meeting of the Ad Club. The program chair also happened to be the founder and president of a highly regarded advertising agency. She instantly "got" genera-tional strategy, asked me to train her agency team in it, and firmly believed I was strapped to a rocket ship that was about to leave the launch pad. She asked me point-blank if I had enough money and talent support to ramp up my consulting practice as swiftly as she somehow knew I would need to do in order to meet the coming demand. I didn't.

And so visionary and entrepreneurial and delightful Maureen Odioso Godshall threw her ad agency behind my fledgling enterprise, and she personally became a financial partner. And off we went.

As the consulting and speaking assignments began to pick up steam in the ensuing months, I needed to formally incorporate my company and give it a name. I had been entitling my speeches "The Generational Imperative," making the point that understanding generational dynamics is no longer an *option* for American business; it's now *imperative* training for everyone. So when the incorporation occurred, and after considering many alternative company names, my original speech title still said it most accurately. And, so it is:

The Generational Imperative, Inc. TGI.

To all those mentioned above, especially to the bold generational theorists and generous friends Strauss and Howe, whose seminal history book helped to pour the foundation for this field of study, and to the many other contributors unmentioned here but who know who they are, heartfelt thanks.

Here's the final piece of *the story behind the story* and the explanation behind this book's subtitle.

At virtually every training event or keynote speech I present to business audiences around the United States and Canada, individual audience members constantly – *constantly* – stop by the podium afterward or e-mail me or write the exact same thought in their formal evaluations of my presentations:

This is terrific business information, but I also can't stop applying your information to my own personal life! I can't wait to get home to talk to my kids, my spouse, my parents, my grandparents, my best friend. I just learned something about them – and us, and me! – that I never understood. You've just changed my life and my family!

So, as the book's subtitle suggests...

This book is meant for the living room, as well as the conference room.

For the bedroom, as well as the boardroom.

For the family reunion, as well as the national convention.

For parent and child, as well as boss and subordinate.

For former classmate, as well as current co-worker.

Thank you, America's generations. You wrote your own fascinating stories – moment by moment, value by value, decision by decision, experience by experience, through the decades. In my consulting and speaking, and now in this book, I simply – and humbly – attempt to connect the dots, hopefully in a way you haven't experienced before.

And to the G.I. generation:

American business has asked me to write this book, and with most of you retired, the workplace and marketplace now focus primarily upon the other four generations, as this book will. But make no mistake; your generation's larger-than-life influence is woven into the lives of the Silents, Boomers, Xers, and Millennials. You remain the yardstick by which all other generations measure their own contributions to life on this planet. Largely because of you, we will always remember the twentieth century as *America's Century*. It remains to be seen whether the younger generations are up to the Herculean task of trying to match your achievements as they take their own leadership turns in the twenty-first.

You are an astonishing generation.

WHAT HIS CLIENTS WRITE ABOUT CHUCK UNDERWOOD

"Beyond the power of the generational message itself, you need to know that Chuck is an absolutely outstanding presenter. If you haven't experienced it yet, you will notice that any room he speaks in becomes absolutely silent while he is weaving the story of each American generation's coming of age and how it has set them attitudinally for life. The crowd does not want him to stop talking. It's an amazing thing I have not seen accomplished by any other speaker on the business circuit.

And now, Chuck weaves that same magic throughout this book. You'll find out soon enough how riveting a "read" this is.

But until you've heard and seen Chuck "live," you haven't fully experienced his spellbinding storytelling.

Here are just a few of the thousands of formal written evaluations of Chuck's presentations by individual clients and audience members."

Maureen Odioso Godshall
Senior Vice President/Account Group Director
Focus/FGW Advertising, Inc.

"The Best"

- You are definitely the front-runner when it comes to the topic of generational studies. *Toledo*

- The best distinction of the different generations I've learned and seen. *Stevenson, WA*

- Best presentation on generational marketing that I have ever heard. *Sacramento*

- Better than excellent. *Denver*

- The best seminar I have ever attended. *Cincinnati*

- Best session I've ever attended at ANY conference – awesome! Captivating! *Chicago*

- Best, most fascinating presentation I have heard in years! *Dallas*

- Best speaker/presenter on any subject I have heard in several years. *Amelia Island*

- Best presentation I've seen at any conference – I just wanted more! *Tampa*

- Best speaker in 12 years of attending training sessions. *Dayton*

- Best talk of the whole week. *Chicago*

- Best one I've seen! Super speaker! Interesting and useful! *Des Moines*

- Best session I've ever attended. *Columbus*

- Out of all the speakers I've listened to, Chuck has been the best. *Davenport*

- I was at a table with seven others and
  they all agreed that yours was the best
  Ad Club presentation they'd seen.   *Lexington*

- Awesome speaker, awesome topic –
  very interesting and relevant!   *Tampa*

- Super speaker! Best one I've seen!
  Interesting and useful!   *Des Moines*

- I attended your speech in Hollywood
  last night. Fannnnnntastic!   *Los Angeles*

- Mr. Underwood was fantastic.   *Palm Springs*

- Underwood – totally outstanding!   *Anaheim*

- I have the attention span of a gnat.
  However, this presentation was one
  of the best and most captivating
  I have ever attended.   *Seaside, OR*

- I really appreciate how sensitively
  Chuck handled tricky topics like
  racism and female denigration.   *Salt Lake City*

"Blown away"

- I am blown away – I could have
  listened all day. Excellent!   *Tampa*

- I could listen to him all day.   *Columbus*

- Everyone at the conference was
  blown away by Chuck Underwood.   *Seattle*

"Phenomenal"

- I thought Underwood's presentation
  was phenomenal.   *Indianapolis*

- Your presentation was phenomenal.   *Orlando*
- Chuck Underwood was a phenomenal presenter. The topic is so interesting and relevant.   *Longmont, CO*

"Researched and Expert"

- It's obvious that Underwood has taken a great deal of time doing research.   *Sacramento*
- Absolutely a great speaker with a deep and well-researched insight and knowledge in strategies of generational marketing.   *Cincinnati*
- The instructor is obviously an expert on his topic.   *Palm Springs*

"Profound"

- It is about as profound an impact as any four-hour seminar could have!   *Grand Rapids*
- Profoundly important information. I'm 47, a boomer. Excellent presentation!   *Chicago*
- Profound perspective.   *Columbia, SC*

WHAT BUSINESS AUDIENCES HAVE WRITTEN ABOUT THE IMPACT OF CHUCK UNDERWOOD'S PRESENTATIONS ON THEIR *PERSONAL LIVES*

- Wow! What an eye-opener. I guess I had no idea what has contributed to Gen X core values…and I have a daughter Gen Xer!   *Columbus*

- I was born in '58. When you spoke of the second wave of Boomers, it was like seeing my life pass before my eyes. Uncanny.   *Cincinnati*

- It's given me a much greater understanding of my Gen X husband and two millennial children!   *Grand Rapids*

- To hear a young man speak so knowledgeably about times and occurrences during his "grandmother's" days was awesome. I felt like I relived part of my life just listening to you.   *Providence*

- At 36, I am a Generation X baby. Hands down, Vietnam and the '70s and divorce rate affected my life more than anything else did. If we are the "divorce" generation, we are also the original "Deadbeat Dad" generation. My dad still owes my mom money. What is it like to wear a $150 pair of shoes? I have no idea.   *St. Petersburg*

- This presentation offers a great platform for those in specific age groups – such as elderly dealing with facing end-of-life (or late-in-life) decisions & involving the families. *Salt Lake City*

- It is truly amazing the way you can broadstroke 59 million people (Gen X) in a generation and get it so right. I was fascinated…. *Cincinnati*

- You have even helped me understand something about my daughter that I may not have fathomed before. *Phoenix*

- This hit home and brought back many memories. *Toledo*

- What I learned at this conference will come in handy for my day-to-day life! *Eugene*

- Absolutely a treasure trove of useful information for work and life! *Columbus*

- Your passion for your subject is evident in every sentence and our group loved it. More importantly, they took home a different and very useful context for their staffing issues and personal relationships. *Savannah*

- Your discussion really hit a nerve. Perhaps it is because I just attended my 20th high school reunion. *St. Petersburg*

- Better understanding for peers and all people who surround your life. *St. Louis*

- Excellent! Fascinating! I now understand myself better!!   *Chicago*

- Your presentation on the peculiarities of the generations was the most exciting, interesting, thought-provoking, and enjoyable that I have had the pleasure to experience. You had me completely absorbed.   *Louisville*

- The material is important for everyone to understand. Manager, marketer, parent, or grandparent can all gain a better understanding of how others think and why. Everyone is engaged in the discussion – our room was alive with participation.   *Denver*

- Chuck's presentation hit home and made a lot of sense and gave me a deeper understanding of the generations that are involved in our lives at work and at home.   *Toronto*

TO CONTACT THE GENERATIONAL IMPERATIVE, INC. AND CHUCK UNDERWOOD ABOUT MANAGAMENT AND DEPARTMENTAL TRAINING, CONSULTING, RESEARCH AND KEYNOTES

If your company or organization wants to discuss Generational Marketing and Communications Strategy or Generational Workforce Diversity and Human Resource Strategy, please contact The Generational Imperative in Cincinnati for more information:

WEB: www.genimperative.com

EM: info@genimperative.com

TABLE OF CONTENTS

Chapter 1

What Is This "Generations" Thing?
No longer an option

Imperative Business Training

In American business, we are just now beginning to comprehend – on a widespread basis – the powerful influence of generational values and generational attitudes on Americans' lifestyle preferences, consumer decisions, and career choices.

And understanding this Generations Dynamic has now become imperative training – for management, individual departments, and all employees in American business – in two massive areas of daily business life.

Generational Marketplace Strategy

One area is the American *marketplace* and virtually every element of it, from A to Z:

- Market Research
- Product/Service Development
- Promotion/Event/Publication Creation
- Marketing Research
- Marketing
- Advertising
- Public Relations
- Selling and Relationship Building
- One-on-One Interpersonal Skills
- Customer Service/Patient Care
- Legislative Relations and Campaign Strategy
- Philanthropy, Fundraising, and Volunteerism

Across all industry types, Generational Strategy can and should influence your up-front market research, the development of your products and services and programs and events, your marketing research, and your marketing and advertising and public relations.

Training in Generational Strategy can significantly enhance your selling success and your one-on-one relationships with clients and customers. Within seven days of training, an Account Rep for one of my newspaper clients emailed to her Publisher, "This has already meant more dollars!"

Generational Strategy carries profound potential in such disciplines as public service by our elected officials, legislative relations, campaign strategies, philanthropy and fundraising, and volunteerism. A political consultant at KMK Consulting in Cincinnati who attended my half-day session on Generational Political And Campaign Strategy emailed this to the ad agency that had sponsored the seminar:

"In the future, I believe generational considerations will transcend traditional demographic information in importance. Politicians and political campaigns alike would benefit greatly from this information...."

Generational Strategy should be understood and implemented by every North American individual and business entity, both for-profit and not-for-profit, and across all industries and disciplines whose task is to effectively market to and communicate with the North American masses.

Generational Workplace Strategy

- Manpower Planning
- Compensation and Benefit Planning
- Job Recruitment Advertising
- Screening and Interviewing
- Recruitment and Retention
- Training and Development
- Coaching and Mentoring
- Leadership Training and Development
- Team Building
- Talent Management
- Innovation
- Performance Assessment
- Succession Planning

The second area is the American workplace and human resources, where employers and managers now need to understand each generation's unique core values and attitudes in order to recruit the best employees, retain and engage them, manage them effectively, maximize their fulfillment and thus their productivity, and achieve a better intergenerational understanding and cooperativeness amongst employees of all generations.

Generational Workplace Strategy helps to guide an organization's up-front staff planning, compensation and benefit planning, and the building and maintenance of its workforce via job advertising, screening, interviewing and recruitment.

And in effectively managing them, this strategy can enhance employee training and development, coaching and mentoring, the development of your leaders, team building, talent management, innovation, performance assessment, succession planning, and virtually every other human resource endeavor.

A comprehensive workshop on Generational Workplace Diversity and Human Resource Strategy is now an essential and permanent staple in the training of an organization's current and future management and leaders, as well as all of its employees.

The three "truths"

The good news about this stuff? It's really easy to *get*.

The premise of generational dynamics is simple. It is based upon three well-researched, universally accepted, and easy-to-understand truths:

Truth #1: Between the time we're born and the time we leave the fulltime classroom for adulthood and our career years, usually in our early twenties, we will form most of the core values and beliefs we'll embrace *our entire lives.* What we witness and directly experience as we pass through our formative years, and what we learn from older generations of parents and educators will guide our basic belief system for life. Oh sure, we'll evolve. But those critical core values will remain largely intact. And those people who share the same formative years' times and teachings will by and large share the same core values. *And by sharing the same core values, we will become* a *generation,* or what the intellectuals like to call an "age cohort." And whenever there is a momentous and widespread change in the times and/or teachings that young children are going to absorb in their formative years, a new generation is created.

Truth #2: In the past century, life in America has changed frequently, and often in sharply new directions. Also, according to the U.S. Census Bureau, we are now living thirty years longer on average than we did in the early 1900s. So, for the first time in history, American life expectancy now permits five living generations, each of whose formative years were notably different from the other generations and whose core values, as a result, are also very different.

Truth #3: Our generational core values and attitudes are going to exert astonishing influence over our consumer decisions, career choices, and lifestyle preferences for life. So if marketers want to influence those decisions, and if employers want to maximize their human resources in the workplace, and if Americans want to understand themselves and their families and their fellow Americans, then they must understand each generation's unique core values.

And to understand those unique generational core values, we must first understand *what happened to each generation during its unique formative years.*

Here's the starting point of generational study. Please say hello to America's five living generations:

Name	Born
G.I.	1901 – 1926
SILENT	1927 – 1945
BOOMER	1946 – 1964
GEN X	1965 – 1981
MILLENNIAL	1982 – present time (2007)*

* Regarding the Millennials' birth year brackets: we'll probably find, by approximately 2010 or 2015, that American children who in 2007 were aged two or four or seven or somewhere in that range are experiencing significantly different formative years' times and teachings than those of the oldest Millennials. If that indeed occurs, then those youngsters will actually become the leading edge of America's next legitimate generation.

But we can't predict the future, can we? And so, we in generational study must temporarily live with the uncertainty of not knowing exactly where the Millennials end and our next generation begins.

From one generational scholar to the next, these birth-year brackets listed above might vary, but only slightly. We generational consultants quibble a bit with each other, but we're usually in pretty close agreement.

And yes, if you're one of those who happens to be born "on the cusp" of two generations, you might find that your own core values are a blend of the two generations that wrap around you. If you're a Boomer born in the late '40s but came of age with older siblings from the Silent generation, they might have pulled you up to their generation's values. And conversely, if you're a Gen Xer born in the early '80s and you have younger Millennial siblings, they might have influenced your core values in the direction of their generation. It sometimes can get a little gray at the edges of each generation's birth-year bracket. Here's an example.

On the day I was submitting the manuscript for this book to the publisher, I received this e-mail from a "cusp'er" who had attended my generational presentation a few days earlier to a national conference of "community leader" associations:

"Dear Chuck, I felt compelled to send you this e-mail to say thank you. I was in the audience last Saturday when you addressed the group at the CLA (Community Leadership Association) Conference in Grand Rapids, MI. Your presentation was a major personal *Ah-ha* moment for me. I've always felt a bit confused about who I am and where I fit in. After listening to you, I realized that it is because I am right on that cusp between being a boomer and a Gen Xer. Understandably then, with two such different generations pulling at me, I am bound to be a bit confused. The thing I want to thank you for is that after you went through your info, I realized that I have the benefit of the best of the characteristics of both of these generations. So thank you for helping me feel a little less confused, and very good about myself."

Beware

This is perhaps the best place in the book to offer a few "alerts" about generational study:

Beware # 1 - end of the Millennials: Regrettably, there are some people out there who are proclaiming, in 2007, that the Millennials end at some specific current age, say age three or six, or seven. But every legitimate generational scholar I know will tell you it's impossible, in 2007, to make any such claim as to where the Millennials end, because we can't possibly know for certain what the remainder of their formative years will bring. If the times and teachings remain similar to the past twenty years, they'll be Millennials. If the times and/or teachings change significantly, they'll become the leading edge of our next generation. *We can't predict the future.*

Beware # 2 - mini-generations that *aren't*: Generational consulting has only recently become a researched and legitimate field of study and, thus, a hot career pursuit. And the inevitable outcome is that a few people are lunging into the profession and subdividing valid generations into invalid mini-generations-that-aren't, or trying to sell bombastic-proclamations-that-aren't in order to sell a book or land a speaking gig. Not only that, the print media love to attach the word "generation" to just about any conceivable micro-segment of our population: GenerationNext, Generation Y, Generation Net, The Whatever Generation, MySpace Generation, Echo Boom Generation, YouTube Generation, Zoomer Generation, Sandwich Generation, and on and on. It's been going on for years. But the fact is, the word "generation" now has a clear definition and so *should* be used accordingly. But the term will probably continue to be abused. Beware of mini-generations-that-aren't-generations. As we near the end of the 2000s, the A-List generational consultants will tell you there are five legitimate generations of living Americans.

Beware # 3 - generation-specific advocacy: A few are getting into generational consulting more as *advocates* and cheerleaders for their own generation than as objective and legitimate research-based consultants. If you want a generational cheerleader, that's fine. But the damage that generational *advocacy*, when masked as consulting, can do to your business is terrifying. Beware the crusaders.

Beware # 4 - the dreaded "online survey": Statistically valid generational research is growing in importance, but beware of consultants and authors who conduct online surveys that aren't properly controlled. Oftentimes, they post surveys on their own Web sites and simply solicit responses from visitors whose identities cannot possibly be confirmed. Such surveys might sound impressive – *we surveyed twenty-thousand Boomers before writing this book* or *for this report* – but the findings might also put you out of business if you rely upon them.

The bottom line:

- Choose your generational consultant wisely and demand legitimacy and objectivity.
- Read generational books, including this one, with a critical eye and force the author to document the content and clearly label any *personal opinions* – in contrast to researched fact – as just that.

What about Canada?
Brothers and sisters, not merely neighbors

Does the content of this book apply to Canadians, or just U.S. citizens? In 2006, I didn't know the answer for certain but needed to find it.

I was asked to come to Toronto to present my half-day session on Generational Workforce Diversity and Human Resource Strategy to about 250 representatives of the Ontario Nurses Association, which represents some fifty thousand nurses in that province. In advance, I hired an experienced marketing researcher to help me to study Canada's generations before I prepared my seminar content. Then, in the question-answer session after the presentation, I point-blank asked the Canadian audience if they felt my content, which they had just heard, was accurate. They also answered this question in their formal written evaluations of the session.

Thankfully, the research and their responses jibed: America's five living generations are very similar in their age brackets, formative years' experiences, and core values to English-speaking Canada, but with a few notable differences.

Canada's G.I. Generation experienced the Great Depression and World War II, which American G.I.s also experienced. Canadian Silents and American Silents experienced the same postwar prosperity and Happy Days. Both countries' Boomers experienced the same social activism of the sixties. Canadian and American Xers felt the sting of their parents' rising divorce rates, permissive parenting, and increasingly cynical and vulgar media. And likewise, both nations' Millennials have come of age with similar times and teachings, including a resurgence of the strong nuclear family, a sense of empowerment and optimism, but also a fear for their physical safety in this era of global terrorism, school shootings, and natural disasters.

A couple of the major differences: At times, these two nations have had sharply different generational experiences with their respective governments. When Canadians have been pleased with their government, Americans have not been pleased with theirs. And vice versa.

Another difference is race relations between each nation's majority and its various minorities, with the issues and historical timelines being occasionally different.

When I recently presented a series of workshops in Baltimore to the annual conference of the Jewish Community Centers of North America, Canada sent a number of delegates who afterward agreed with the same conclusion I've reached from my research:

Americans and Canadians are too similar in their generational values and beliefs to consider each other mere "neighbors." Instead, we seem to be more like brothers and sisters.

Translation? Like brothers and sisters, we are free to develop our own unique and distinctive personalities and do things our own way. We will sometimes disagree with each other.

But we have such a strong "shared center" or "common core" from similar formative years' times and teachings that our two countries' generations pretty much embrace the same core values and basic beliefs.

But you Canadians can read on and decide for yourselves.

What about other nations?
Does this stuff apply?

No.

Most of my clients ask this question, especially the ones involved in international business. I advise them that the Generational Strategy I present in training sessions – and in this book – is trustworthy in the United States and English-speaking Canada. In all other countries, I explain, generational research specific to those other countries is needed. England and Australia are *close*, but I'd rather advise my clients on the side of caution.

How about immigrants?

What about immigrants to North America? Hispanics, Asians, Europeans, and others?

The simplified answer regarding all immigrants to the United States or English-speaking Canada boils down to this:

How many of an immigrant's all-important formative years – roughly the first twenty years of his or her life – did the immigrant spend living in the United States or Canada?

Let's say you were born in 1970. Your family emigrated from, say, Mexico or Japan or India to the United States *when you were three or four years old.* Assuming your parents encouraged you to embrace American culture and use the English language, then you almost certainly are now a card-carrying member of Gen X, because you will have *experienced the same formative years' times and teachings* as your American peers.

But, if you came to America when you were in your very late teens or early twenties, meaning you missed Xers' formative years that molded their unique and lifelong core values, then you will *never* be a member of that generation.

If you moved here at age ten? Yes, you're probably a member, because we tend to mold our lifelong core values in two big chunks: in the first ten to twelve years of our lives, we assimilate the values that come primarily from our parents and family members; then, in the second half of our formative years, we start to add the core values that come from our peers, as we begin to stand on our own and make our own judgments.

Is there one specific cutoff age that determines whether immigrants are, or are not, full-fledged members of their American generation? No. The later in your formative years you came here, the less likely you are to be a member.

It's a sliding scale.

When it comes to defining generations, *formative years' times and teachings* are everything.

Does generational strategy work with children aged two to seventeen?

No. At least not fully. And in my opinion, not to a trustworthy extent.

Generational core values don't become fully developed – and reliable – until we reach *about* age seventeen and graduate from high school. Additional values will become solidified and credible by our early twenties. For marketers and employers that wish to get into the heads of kids younger than seventeen, I advise my clients to not use generational strategy. Instead, I advise them to rely upon *age*-based research.

Generational Core Values = Marketing Hot Buttons
Generational Core Values = Workplace Alerts

It's simple:

In the marketplace, generational core values are the equivalent of *hot buttons* that marketers can push to effectively influence and persuade whichever generation they choose to target.

In the workplace, generational core values are beneficial *alerts* that can help employers to identify potential employee strengths and shortcomings and enhance those employers' abilities to recruit, retain, engage, manage, and maximize the productivity of all employees from the various generations. And when employees are trained in generational differences, the generation gaps shrink, thus enhancing understanding and cooperativeness amongst all employees.

When it comes to understanding generational differences, *core values* are everything.

And in order to understand each generation's core values, we must understand what happened to each generation during its unique formative years.

We must take a stroll down Memory Lane.

With that, it's time to get into the heads of the four American generations that are of vital importance to the American marketplace and workplace....

Chapter 2

The Silents
Our nation's last innocent generation

FORMATIVE YEARS, CORE VALUES, ADULTHOOD, FUTURE

Born: 1927 - 1945
46,582,000 born
Formative years: early '30s to early '60s

The Silent Generation.

As *consumers* today, they are richer, freer spending, less brand loyal, and more receptive to advertising and to new products than the generations that previously occupied their current age bracket. A long list of marketers is pursuing this generation. And as we'll see, some are pitching the Silents in order to get to their Millennial grandchildren and great-grandchildren.

As *employees* today, many Silents are working beyond the traditional retirement age, at least part-time, and smart employers are aggressively recruiting and retaining Silents because this generation's skills and wisdom and maturity are needed more than ever and can be especially beneficial to younger coworkers.

Now then, let's head down Memory Lane.

The Silent Generation is described as the generation born too late to be World War II heroes and too soon to immerse themselves in the social activism of the 1960s.

Silents are *very* small in number – just under forty-seven million born, according to the U.S. Census Bureau. Why? Because their birth years occur primarily during the Great Depression, when conceiving another mouth to feed is often economically unwise, and during World War II, when it is kind of *logistically difficult* to conceive a child because sixteen million young American men are overseas saving the world.

Great Depression
World War II
The American High

Three major periods dominate the all-important formative years of Silent kids and will mold the unique core values that will guide this generation's decision making for life:

1. the struggle and sacrifice – but also the community cooperation - of the Great Depression;
2. followed by the horror – but then the triumph – of World War II;

3. followed by the odd coexistence of the Cold War threat and yet one of the most joyous periods in our country's history for most, but not all Americans: the so-called American High or Happy Days of the post-war period, from 1946 to 1962.

Young Silent kids are coming of age, if you can imagine this, when it is actually uncool to be young. Our nation is not yet worshipping youth.

G.I. Joe and Rosie the Riveter

Instead, the celebrities – the heroes – of American life are twenty-something, thirty-something, and forty-something G.I. Generation men and the millions of G.I. Generation women (I've seen estimates that range from 6,000,000 to 18,000,000) who rush into the labor force during the war and contribute greatly to our nation's astonishing war-time production, becoming collectively known as *Rosie the Riveter*. Without fully appreciating it at the time, they set the stage for the modern feminist movement that will emerge twenty years hence.

The Silent kids are not jealous of the older G.I. Generation. They worship them too.

Russell Baker, a Pulitzer Prize-winning journalist, speaks for most young boys who were too young to fight when he writes this after the war:

"I hated the war ending. I wanted desperately to become a death-dealing hero. I wanted the war to go on and on."

Japan surrenders

But World War II ends in August 1945 when the Japanese surrender. And so the Silents are going to come of age beneath the gigantic, glowing shadow of the older G.I. Generation, whose men are now returning from overseas and pouring back in to domestic life and whose women are, by and large, relinquishing their wartime jobs to the men and returning to homemaking.

The Silent kids' respect for – and deference to – the G.I. Generation are showing up on the job, in the college classroom, down at the corner tavern, everywhere.

The G.I. Generation, from its unique formative years' experiences, is effervescing with confidence, enthusiasm, boldness, vision, and leadership-leadership-leadership.

The younger Silent Generation kids are coming of age comparatively *quiet.*

Historian William Manchester would later write this about the Silents, and this is the quote most often credited with giving this generation its eternal name:

"Never had American youth been so withdrawn, cautious, unimaginative, indifferent, unadventurous, and silent."

Cold War threat
McCarthyism
Suburbs
The American Way!

As young Silents are forming their all-important core values, events are taking place that have their parents and educators teaching Silent children to CONFORM.

Remember the word "conform." This is an era marked forever by its extreme and, to many Silent youths, *suffocating* conformity. Why?

- The Cold War is on, so in America this is not a time for dissent or serious protest against our nation's major institutions. Instead, Americans set aside domestic disagreements in order to demonstrate absolute national solidarity against the new and significant military threat from the Soviet Union.
- McCarthyism, the later-damned "Communist witch hunt" spearheaded by Wisconsin Senator Joseph McCarthy, is spreading a fear of speaking out against anything American.
- And there's this: an American attitude that we now want – and desperately need, after sixteen years of depression and war – to enjoy and demonstrate to the entire world the freedom, prosperity, and lifestyle that our men and women have just fought so valiantly, and at such staggering human cost, to preserve. We need to smile and laugh and renew our spirit.

So, their parents are *patriotically* displaying their sudden postwar prosperity, Silent kids are happily behaving in the *World's Finest Classrooms*, everyone is exalting in the American Way, and no one is rocking the boat.

Well, almost no one.

Whenever there is an *extreme* in America, frequently a few rebel against it. And in this era of conformity, a handful of Silent kids will react with a fierce commitment to *rock the hell out of the boat*: feminist crusader Gloria Steinem; consumer advocate Ralph Nader; TV pioneer Phil Donahue; civil rights leader Martin Luther King, Jr.; entertainer Elvis Presley; business visionary Ted Turner; the "Beat" writers like Jack Kerouac and Alan Ginsberg; and other mold breakers. They will launch a full frontal assault on the conformity of their own generation's formative years and, by doing so, help to effect profound change in American life, especially in another decade or so when the younger Boomers add their passion and masses and idealism to this quest for a better America.

The American High
1946 to 1962

Try to imagine what young Silents are experiencing as they come of age during this wondrous postwar American High:

- Peace, after a war in which some 406,000 Americans lost their lives.
- Job security for Dad and prosperity for many, after sixteen grinding years of depression and war.
- Home ownership for the family, unattainable for many until now.
- The invention of this thing called *television*, which will turn American life inside out.
- Discovery of the vaccine that virtually eradicates the horrible disease, polio.

- The joyful explosion of national interest in American automobiles, which are suddenly big and flashy and brightly colored and seem to mirror the optimism and hope of the American people in this post-Depression and postwar glow.

And with cars now affordable to most Americans, other related industries are created during the American High:

- Motels, instead of just downtown hotels.
- And with motels being rapidly constructed alongside the nation's roadways comes a new phenomenon: the *family driving vacation,* which all of those G.I. Generation fathers insist must begin with a wake-up call to the wife and kids at 4 a.m.! And, from 1955 to 1963, Americans are encouraged every Saturday night on national TV by singer Dinah Shore to take that driving vacation. She closes her hugely popular variety show with her legendary jingle, *"See the USA in Your Chevrolet,"* which *Ad Age* magazine, forty years later, will rate as the fifth-best advertising jingle of the twentieth century. Here are the lyrics:

> "Seeeeeeeee the U.S.A.
> In your Chevolet,
> America is asking you to call.
> Drive your Chevrolet
> Through the U.S.A.,
> America's the greatest land of all!"

- With automobiles suddenly everywhere, drive-in movie theatres are suddenly everywhere. And for many Silent kids coming of age after the war, the drive-in date becomes Saturday Night America.

- During this magical American High, construction of the interstate highway system begins. It is the largest earth-moving project in the history of the planet. Ultimately, it will mean more than 46,000 miles of pavement, connecting us Americans and pulling us more closely together, both physically and psychologically.
- The Silents can now listen to the radio *while walking down the street* because of the invention, right after the war, of the tiny transistor, and with it, the small handheld and battery-powered transistor radio, immortalized forever by the early-'60s song by Freddy Boom Boom Cannon, "Transistor Sister." Lyrics: *"If you got it right... you get no static... the time and weather is automatic... my transistor sister... playing her radio!"*
- AM-radio disc jockeys are larger-than-life celebrities as Silent kids come of age. The DJs are upbeat, optimistic, and clean talking.
- *Playboy* magazine arrives in 1953, and Silent boys suddenly discover additional storage space in their bedrooms: under the mattress! The Silent Generation, incidentally, is labeled our nation's Last Innocent Generation, and our nation's Most Sexually Frustrated Generation. The birth control pill hasn't yet arrived, and Silent girls are expected to "save" themselves for their wedding night (and then, somehow, instantly be expert in lovemaking).

In 2001, I produced and hosted a public television talk show special, with a live studio audience, that was all about the Silent Generation. One of our featured onstage Silent-Generation guests was Nick Clooney, the handsome and intellectual father of handsome actor George Clooney. On the show, we talked about all things Silent, and when we got to the part about this being the "most sexually frustrated generation" a half century earlier, Nick joked, "We still are!"

Silent Generation girls, in their poodle skirts and saddle shoes, are coming of age watching their mothers around the house, and they see Mom rejoicing in a sudden blizzard of newly invented and affordable household conveniences. Right before her eyes:

- The American home is evolving from hand-crank wringer-washer machines, one sock or T-shirt at a time, to *automatic* washers!
- From hanging wet clothes on a backyard line, if the weather permits, to simply tossing them into an *automatic* dryer down in the basement!
- From meals that were always made every day from scratch – hours at a time – to these newfangled pop-'em-in-the-oven *TV dinners* (as the label on Swanson's TV dinner packages read, "MMmmm – it's good for you")!
- From having just the audio of radio as Mom's daytime companion during her homemaking hours to now having real-life moving images on this magical thing called TV!
- And, from major appliances that used to come only in white to a choice of *three* colors! Additional colors would soon follow. When I present generational seminars to live audiences around the country, I always ask the audience members if they remember the other two colors. Invariably, every woman who is a First-Wave Boomer or older instantly remembers. They shout, "Avocado Green!" and "Harvest Gold!" Some add, "Turquoise!" It's more than a half century later and we remember appliance colors! But these were the fabulous times of the American High.

Homemaking is suddenly a wondrous experience, and the American housewife is *celebrated* every week in national magazines, which are enormously influential during the American High.

This is a period of raging materialism. "Things" are uncommonly important because Americans have just gone without a lot of things during sixteen years of depression and war.

And because these are their formative years, Silents will go through their entire lives placing a special value on "things," on their possessions.

And a half century later, smart marketers are seizing upon this strong core value of the Silent generation.

Silent girls

During their formative years, Silent girls are expected to graduate from high school, marry, bear children, and then stay at home to raise them.

If they go to college, even the college administrators assume they're there for one purpose, and these three words are burned forever into the memory of many Silent females: *find a husband.*

On that same television talk show mentioned above, one onstage Silent female guest was Julia Maxton, now the president of a regional Chamber of Commerce. She described her first day at college back in the early fifties:

"All students filed into the gymnasium. Against one wall of the gym was a row of small desks, where counselors sat. The students lined up single file in front of these desks. Boys in one line, girls in the other, boys, girls. One by one, we sat at the desk and mapped out our entire four-year academic curriculum with the counselor. Each of the boys got a half hour or longer with the counselor. Each girl got about sixty seconds. My counselor told me, 'Just major in liberal arts and take horseback riding, because we know you're here to *find a man.*'"

Only a couple of professions are widely available to Silent girls coming of age: primarily, teaching and nursing, or perhaps selling this newly invented product line of food-storage containers called Tupperware at neighborhood living room parties, which are great fun during the American High.

So in this environment, Silents become the youngest marrying and youngest child-bearing generation in modern U.S. history.

Silent marriage
Average age, women:	**20**
Average age, men:	**23**
Average # of kids:	**3.3**

Silent women marry at the average age of twenty, the men are twenty-three, and together they will bear a whopping 3.3 children per couple.

African-American Silents
Struggle
Northern migration
Hopeful drumbeats

American negroes – they are not yet referring to themselves as African-Americans and blacks – are struggling.

These are not the same Happy Days for people of color as for white Americans. Hatred and oppression and violence are everywhere.

But during this postwar period, they do see a few rays of sunshine finding their way through our nation's racist clouds:

It is during this time that Southern blacks accelerate the largest mass migration in U.S. history, as some five million of them move from working primarily as sharecroppers in the South to industrial jobs in booming postwar Northern cities like Chicago, Detroit, and Cleveland. A portion of them begin a westward migration to cities such as Kansas City and, ultimately, on out to the Coast.

Because of the miracle of television and its news footage, the whole nation – black and white – now vividly *sees* the true ugliness of racism and, with it, *the first hopeful drumbeats of civil rights:*

- In 1947, Jackie Robinson breaks baseball's color barrier, and in 1950, Earl Lloyd and several others do the same in pro basketball, and so blacks slowly begin to get their chance in professional sport.

- In 1948, Congress integrates our nation's military forces.
- Also in the '40s, Pepsi Cola acknowledges the importance of the "Negro market" by hiring black sales executives to sell its soft drink to vendors and to pose as models in its commercial ads.
- In 1954, we get Brown v. the Board of Education, the famous Supreme Court ruling on school desegregation, striking down the doctrine of separate but equal that had been in place since Plessy v. Ferguson in 1896.
- In 1955, a tiny black seamstress decides "enough is enough," refuses to give up her seat on an overcrowded Alabama bus to a white man as the law mandates she must, gets arrested, and so begins the Rosa Parks-inspired Montgomery bus boycott.
- Young black Silents are coming of age reading the increasingly strident writings of black authors like Ralph Ellison, James Baldwin, and Langston Hughes.
- They hear the early voice of the Dexter Avenue Baptist Church minister, who was born "Michael" but whose father would change the name of his son, at age five, to Martin Luther King, Junior.
- Black entertainers like Nat King Cole, Harry Belafonte, and Sammy Davis, Junior, are starting to show up on TV and become an important source of pride for Americans of color.
- And on radio – and this will be noteworthy – *white* teenage Silents are enthusiastically embracing the black recording artists who are singing a new, uninhibited, and boisterous type of music that some older white Americans angrily and hatefully denounce as devil music and demon music and worse (one newspaper headline even proclaims it a "communicable

disease") before it gets its permanent name in the early 1950s from white Cleveland radio disc jockey Alan Freed, who calls this new music *rock 'n roll*. Sometimes against their elders' wishes, those white Silent kids dig in their heels, purchase this music, and dance to it at mixed-race nightclubs where black bands are onstage playing it. And so pop music becomes an important bridge between black and white America. And because these are their formative years, the music influences the Silents' lifelong core values, which explains why this generation will eventually be labeled a rights-oriented and "inclusive" generation.

So, a few rays of sunshine, but the modern Civil Rights Movement – the Glorious Struggle, as the '60s will come to be known – is still years away for Silent Generation blacks coming of age.

War/prosperity
Suffocating conformity
Racism/chauvinism
Joy of being an American

So the Silent Generation forms its unique and lifelong core values during a time of war but then prosperity, a suffocating conformity, racism, chauvinism – it wasn't yet called sexism – and materialism.

But this is also an era of uncommon community cooperation, low crime rates, job stability for the majority, and the overwhelming joy – after the triumph of World War II and the peace that follows – of being an American.

The core values that Silents have just formed, based upon what they've just experienced and been taught by their elders as they've come of age, are now going to influence their consumer decisions, career choices, and lifestyle preferences *for a lifetime.*

Adulthood for Silents
The Organization Man
"Born too soon"

Here, big picture, is how adulthood plays out for the Silents.

The Silent Generation, by definition, begins to graduate from high school right at the end of World War II and, also by definition, does not fight in that war (with a few exceptions, who patriotically lie about their birth dates and enlist underage).

Although the Silents will have "their generation's war" – the Korean Conflict from 1950 to 1953 – the timing nonetheless can't be much better for this generation to begin its career passage.

For the white Silent male entering adulthood in this exciting era of sudden prosperity, the company becomes an extension of the man's own personality. He becomes *The Organization Man*, as the 1956 William Whyte book is entitled (subtitle, "The book that defined a generation"), or *The Man in the Grey Flannel Suit,* as the 1956 Sloan Wilson book and, later, the Gregory Peck movie is named.

"The corporation came first."

Acclaimed journalist and author David Halberstam, in an important book entitled *The Fifties*, writes these words about the corporate culture of General Motors in the 1950s. And during this era, General Motors is *the* yardstick against which most other major American corporations measure their own culture and performance.

"The men who ran the corporation were square and proud of it. Loyalty among employees was more important than individual brilliance. Team players were valued more highly than mavericks. The corporation came first. The individual was always subordinated to the greater good of the company."

And in 1958, also chronicled in *The Fifties*, Ray Kroc, who was then working with the McDonald brothers in California to roll out the nation's first fast-food franchises, sent a now famous memo to the brothers, which said this, in part:

"We have found out that we cannot trust some people who are nonconformists. We will make conformists out of them in a hurry. You cannot give them an inch. The organization cannot trust the individual; the individual must trust the organization."

So, in this business environment of extreme conformity, the message from the corporation to that aspiring young white Silent male is very clear: work hard, be absolutely loyal to the organization, do it our way, don't rock the boat, pay your dues, and if you do all of that, you'll eventually be *entitled to reward*.

And after those sixteen years of depression and war, that message sounds absolutely delicious.

So, the young white Silent career man pledges that absolute loyalty, conforms to the company's way of doing business, works diligently and hard, and conducts himself with a very careful political correctness before *political correctness* was even a buzzword.

And because the economy is flourishing as he begins his work years, and because Silent blacks and females are largely excluded from the better jobs and promotion paths, and because this generation is so tiny in number when demand for workers is so great, *the white Silent male receives the smoothest career ride of any generation of worker in modern American history.* It all *works* for the overwhelming majority of white Silent males. And so they understandably embrace this kind of workplace culture.

The Great American Corporate Meltdown

However, this combination of absolute loyalty to the company and that strong sense of entitlement – *I will be entitled to reward* – contribute to what *The Wall Street Journal,* decades later, would describe as the great American corporate "meltdown" of 2002.

White Silent males begin advancing into corporate America's executive suites in the early 1980s, as the last of the older G.I. Generation executives retire and hand the leadership baton to the next generation.

And, according to the calculations of Arthur Levitt, longest-serving chairman of the Securities and Exchange Commission, this is precisely when the corruptive mindset, the corruptive culture, begins.

As Mr. Levitt said on CNN just as the Enron and WorldCom and many other executive scandals were surfacing in 2002, the belief that this executive corruption is "merely a few bad apples" is sadly mistaken.

Our nation has had, he calculated in that interview, "fifteen to twenty years" of unethical culture coming out of the executive suites, where the prevailing executive attitude among far too many white Silent male executives has been *absolutely anything for the company* (even if unethical and illegal), and *I've paid my dues, always did as I was told, and, by god, I'm now entitled to reward!"*

One important point: As the executive scandals have surfaced, there are a number of Boomers – and even a Gen Xer or two – accused and convicted of wrongdoing too. No generation has cornered the market on corruption and greed. But the corruption has occurred during the era when the Silents occupied the nation's leadership positions in business, government, religion, media, education, sport, and virtually every other major institution, when the policy making and decision making have been largely dictated downward by this subset, the white male executive, of this otherwise ethical and noble generation.

As you'll read, each generation has its successes and failures, and the executive greed-and-corruption epidemic of the '80s, '90s, and now into the 2000s will forever rest in the lap of that white Silent male. Not every one of them. But enough of them to have a profound impact on American life.

History will record the era of the '80s, '90s, and 2000s as the Era of Executive Excess, which has alienated many middle Americans and – as you'll read with the young Millennials – is now giving us a generation that appears to be growing up to be anti-executive greed, pro-worker, and probably pro-union.

Silent women in adulthood

The Silent Generation woman in adulthood:

As former United Nations Ambassador Jeane Kirkpatrick once said, "We are the generation born twenty years too soon."

Too soon to catch two waves that younger Boomer women would catch in another decade or two: the invention of the birth control pill, which first hits the market in 1960 but won't enjoy widespread use until the mid- to late-'60s; and, the feminist movement, which gains major propulsion in the '60s.

Most Silent girls had passed through their formative years fully anticipating an adulthood as homemakers. Remember, corporate America wasn't letting them into the workplace back then, except in nursing, teaching, secretarial work, and a few other tiny pockets of the workplace. So these young girls were told – today, this is unimaginable – to be *grateful* if and when they received a marriage proposal, because it might otherwise be financially difficult for them to live on their own.

But beginning in the mid-1960s, two events force many of them to find jobs and careers.

First of all, The Sexual Revolution is underway. Most Silents are already married when it hits, but those younger, sexually liberated Boomer girls – with access to The Pill – have given many men of ALL generations a case of what several authors will later describe as "Jennifer Fever."

And in 1971, according to U.S. Census Bureau figures, the divorce rate is 165 percent higher than it had been only ten years earlier!

Secondly, the feminist movement is now creating, especially among those First-Wave Boomer couples who are entering adulthood, the dual-career-income household, as young adult women get their first widespread shot at real careers rather than just "jobs." And these dual-career-income households swiftly drive up the cost of living for all Americans.

So Silent women, most now in their thirties and forties, find themselves thrust into the American workplace – either as divorcees on their own, or happily married and simply trying to help their husbands to keep pace with this sudden rise in the cost of living.

Most Silent women are educationally unprepared to compete with younger Boomer women for the skilled positions. And many are psychologically unprepared for this sudden new life: sitting at a desk in an office, rather than standing in the kitchen at home and proudly preparing tonight's family dinner from scratch. It is a traumatic time for many Silent women.

"It's So Nice to Have a Man around the House"

In their generation's formative years, Silent girls had sung along with a Dinah Shore top-twenty hit about married bliss:

"It's So Nice to Have a Man around the House, a knight in shining armor, something of a charmer, put no one else above him, a house is just a house without a man."

That was the '50s. But now in the '70s, Silent women are in the workplace with these aggressive career-minded Boomer feminists, who, in *their* formative years, sang along to Helen Reddy's slightly different lyrics:

"If I have to, I can do anything, I am strong, I am invincible, I am woman."

Hear me roar.

But an interesting thing happens. Those Silent women reach down deep, make the adjustment, and as many of them start to turn forty and fifty, they feel a couple of sensations they never could've imagined for themselves while growing up: financial independence; and, living alone but being okay with it.

They *survive.* And many of them actually flourish in the workplace and become career role models to their own daughters – and sons.

To refer once again to that television talk show special in 2001: a twenty-something Gen X female sat in our studio audience with her divorced Silent mother. Near the end of the show, after listening to the discussion about all of these life passages her mother's generation had gone through, the daughter stood and said, "I was a latchkey kid in the '90s and resented the fact that Mom had to find a job and wasn't 'there' for me like she had been for my older brothers and sisters. But until today, I never realized what she went through when she was forced to work. Now I appreciate her so much more."

And her mother then stood up beside her daughter said, "I would rather have been at home for her after school, to give her warm milk and cookies like I had been able to do with her older brothers and sisters when I was still married. But I had to go to work."

Richest retirees ever
Free spenders
Many will work in retirement
Pent-up desire to live
Feel underappreciated

In retirement, and many Silents are not there yet, this generation will be financially better off than any generation before them.

They spend their money more freely than prior generations. I conducted Silent Generation focus groups in multiple states for a Denver client – one of the world's largest providers of escorted group travel tours – and, boy, did the Silents confirm this during those focus groups: they feel they have *earned the right* to reward themselves. They've worked hard for a lot of years, they've been devoted parents, they did what they were told, they didn't rock the boat, and so *now it's our time. We've earned it!*

A significant number of Silents are working well past retirement age, at least part-time. Many are doing so not so much for the money but instead to stay plugged in and vital, while other Silents must work because the executive corruption scandals, such as Enron and WorldCom, and/or the stock market collapse of 2000 ravaged their retirement nest eggs.

And these extended work years will only increase their importance to the American workplace. And it will increase their purchasing power and, thus, the interest of marketers and advertisers in this generation.

"Apolitical. Safe. Silent. And boring."
"It's now our time...."

As you deal with Silents, you might detect a pent-up desire for adventure, experimentation, taking chances, a desire to *live life.* Here's what that's all about.

Frank Kaiser, a Silent who writes for the Web site SuddenlySenior.com, wrote this about his generation:

"We became apolitical. Safe. Silent. And boring. We didn't save the world like the previous generation, and we didn't squeeze life for all of its satisfactions the way

Boomers have. Like lightning, the realization hit us that we only go around once, and it's now our time to start living it on our terms."

And there's a line in a Bob Dylan song – *My Back Pages* – that also says it perfectly for the current-day Silent mindset:

"I was so much older then, I'm younger than that now."

That Silent core value – that passion to live life – opens up a banquet table of opportunities for marketers and employers.

Five months after the airplane terror attacks of 9/11, I was presenting a training session to a large group of finance industry executives in Washington, D.C. While in town, I read a newspaper story written by a reporter who had contacted travel agents around the country and asked if Americans were returning to air travel vacations in the near aftermath of those four airplane hijackings and crashes. The story said that Boomers and Xers were not yet flying, still hesitant about the safety of air travel.

But the Silents were jumping right back in to leisure travel on planes. They were even flying to violent hot spots such as the Middle East for their vacations!

That Silent Generation core value and consumer attitude were crystal clear with their purchasing decision:

We only go around once, and it's now our time.

Connect with grandchildren
Think and act young
Love to travel

As consumers, the Silents have lots of hot buttons that marketers can push.

Here are just three hot buttons:

1. Silents are especially passionate about being a regular and meaningful presence in the lives of their grandchildren and great-grandchildren.

   Del Webb, the division of Pulte Homes that is the builder of those massive Sunbelt retirement communities like Sun City, Arizona, is now building retirement communities in the cold-weather states, acknowledging the generationally-designed research that documents that many Silent retirees in those regions are staying put in order to be near their kids and grandkids. (By the way, the early indications are Boomers are doing the same as grandparents).

2. Silents feel they conformed and played it safe when they were young, so today they're eager to think and act young and vibrant.

   A recent research study found that 78 percent of Silents feel that being receptive to new products and services is an important part of "thinking young." This statistic suggests that Silents are not as brand loyal as previous generations had been at the same age bracket. And that means Silents are "in play" in the marketing and advertising universe.

3. And Silents love to travel because, when they were children, America did not have the interstate highway system for easy ground travel, and air travel was prohibitively expensive for all but the wealthiest.

So, who's tapping into just this short list of Silent hot buttons? How 'bout Walt Disney World?

In a recent advertising campaign celebrating the 100-year anniversary of the birth of founder Walt Disney, a TV spot shows a Silent grandfather and his preteen grandson at Disney World, staring up at a statue of Walt Disney and Mickey Mouse. Here's the dialogue:

Silent Grandfather: "Do you know who that is?"
Grandson: "Mickey!"
Silent Grandfather: "What about the man?"
(Grandson shrugs, shakes his head.)
"That's Walt Disney, the guy who came up with Mickey Mouse. He dreamed up this whole place. He could take an ordinary day and turn it into magic. He was full of fun ideas."
"Oh... kinda like you, Grandpa."
(They smile and hug).

This spot does not show Grandpa and Grandson merely riding the rides. It shows them talking, Silent grandpa sharing his knowledge of the Disney history with his grandson and still hip enough to connect with his grandson and gain his admiration. A rich relationship. A strong bond.

This is excellent messaging to this generation, which is so passionate about being a *meaningful presence* in their grandchildren's and great-grandchildren's lives.

<u>Globus & Cosmos</u>
Staff seminar
Silent focus groups
New product development
New catalogs and brochures
New advertising

One of my Denver clients is a travel company called Group Voyagers, one of the world's largest providers of escorted group tours, whose two tour brands are Globus & Cosmos, one higher priced than the other.

As the executive director of sales and marketing told me when we first met, the escorted group tour industry had enjoyed a great run with the G.I. Generation; it understood that generation's preferences regarding group travel. But now, he said, the Silents have become the new prime target, with the Boomers right behind them. And he sensed – accurately – that Silents and Boomers will be very different group tour travelers than G.I.s. So here's what we did together.

I trained Group Voyagers' sixteen-person marketing team in Generational Marketing Strategy. Immediately after my last words in the seminar, the executive director asked the team what they thought of Generational Strategy, and they answered that they wanted to use it. The VP turned to me and asked, "What's our next step?"

I asked if Group Voyagers had focus-grouped the Silents. "No," he answered.

So I designed a generation-specific research study, moderated Silent focus groups in multiple states, and presented the final report to Group Voyagers.

Group Voyagers then incorporated the findings into its product development, marketing, and advertising. It revised the copy in its catalogues and brochures, in some cases adjusted the actual hour-by-hour travel schedules on the tours to accommodate new generational core values, and introduced new marketing elements to enhance bottom-line sales. In our focus groups, we tested specific words and phrases in the brochure copy.

Soon after the research project, the executive director e-mailed me:

"Your generational research study for us has been very helpful in directing our planners and marketing people. We will incorporate the findings not only in the creation of tours, but also in how we talk about travel experiences in brochures and ad copy. Thank you!"

And about six months later, he e-mailed again: "Your work with us continues to shape what we do here. Business is finally picking up...."

Wendy's

I had the pleasure to work with Wendy's for five years, producing an annual television special I created for – and with – them. Wendy's primary target demo had always been eighteen to forty-nine. But Wendy's – like Del Webb, an early embracer of generational research – launched an advertising campaign that included a TV spot that effectively targets that Silent Generation core value of being a significant presence in their grandchildren's lives. And this spot stretches Wendy's demographic reach well beyond age forty-nine and below eighteen. Here's the creative:

Teenage granddaughter, with braces on her teeth, walks into the kitchen with a carryout bag of Wendy's. White-haired Silent grandmother awaits her. They sit down together at the kitchen table:

Silent Grandma: "So where ya been?"
Teen Granddaughter: "Out."
"Where'd ya go?"
"Wendy's."
"Wha'd ya get?"
"Junior Bacon Cheeseburger, fries, and Coke."
"Your grandfather and I love that Junior Bacon Cheeseburger. Two strips of bacon, right?"
"Mm-hmm."
"We get a side salad; used to be 99 cents."
"It's still 99 cents."
(Announcer inserts "sell" message).
Grandma (twinkle in eye): "Does that nice blond boy still work there?"
Granddaughter: "No, Gram, not anymore."
"Too bad. He was *hot.*"
"Grandma!!!!"

Silent Generation grandmother is so hip and "with it" she can actually cause her teen granddaughter to blush. Excellent Silent messaging by Wendy's.

Energizer Batteries

Energizer Batteries demonstrated a similar advertising strategy in a recent holiday campaign. At holiday time, wouldn't you think Energizer would target the younger parents of those younger children who are going to get all of those battery-powered toys and games as gifts?

Not this time. Energizer seized upon Silent core values of wanting to (1) think and act young and (2) connect with their grandkids.

The TV spot shows a Silent grandfather and his pudgy preteen grandson, sitting across from each other in over-stuffed living room chairs, each one furiously working his hand-held, battery-powered Bormoto console as they compete against each other in a video game.

White-haired and bespectacled Silent grandfather missed the technology revolution, so grandson keeps beating him, game after game, telling Gramps, "I win, you lose. I win again, you lose. This is getting ugly." And Grandpa is becoming progressively frazzled and discouraged.

But then, the grandson's console – which doesn't use Energizer batteries – begins to slow down. Grandpa, with Energizers that are outlasting his grandson's Brand X batteries, begins to catch up, and he finally wins a game! He shouts, "Yeah!!!" and immediately leaps out of his chair, towers over his seated grandson, raises his arms to the sky and yells "Yeah!" again, and then does a wild, in-your-face victory dance as his grandson slumps in the chair and rolls his eyes. Grandpa taunts, "How do ya like Granddad? How do ya like him now?!!!"

Silent grandfather is so physically vigorous, so youthful, that he can jump from his chair, dance, and rejoice in beating grandson at a game Gramps had never before seen.

Generational core values – that Silent desire to be youthful and vital, and the desire to bond with grandchildren – become advertising hot buttons.

Sony Camcorders

As with Energizer, this was a holiday-time advertising campaign for Sony camcorders. It captured another unique core value of the Silent Generation: a passion to live life fully, to finally take a few risks, to "squeeze life for all of its satisfactions," which many Silents feel they didn't do during their youth-time years of don't-rock-the-boat conformity.

Once again, during the holiday gift-buying season, wouldn't you assume that Sony Camcorders would advertise to young parents who want to tape their infant kids tearing open their gifts?

This sixty-second TV spot begins by showing a white-haired Silent male jogging through a field in an early morning workout, then drinking a protein milkshake for breakfast, then working out at the gym, packing his Sony Camcorder in his suitcase, checking the weather in Moscow online, hugging his Gen X daughter and son and saying goodbye, flying to Moscow, entering a space center facility guarded by stern-looking Russian soldiers, and then blasting off in a Soviet spaceship, and joyously doing a floating back-flip inside the ship in anti-gravity outer space. The on-screen text at the end of the commercial is perfect messaging to a generational core value of *it's now our time*.

"When your kids ask where the money went... show them the tape."

Public television and Doo Wop

Silents have felt overlooked and underappreciated because they're sandwiched between two wave-making generations: the save-the-world, nation-building G.I.s and the social-activist Boomers.

Even *their war* – the Korean Conflict – has always been overshadowed by WW II.

Here's what happened.

A few years back, public television stations aired a single, two-hour music concert that showcases a style of music that is indigenous to the formative years of the Silents: the '40s and '50s and very early '60s.

Makes strategic sense. Silents now occupied the "sweet spot" of the demographic that public TV targets for call-in donations during its "pledge campaigns."

The stations aired this concert during a pledge campaign. The concert was called, simply, *Doo Wop*.

I learned later from T.J. Lubinsky, the creator and

executive producer of *Doo Wop*, that the previous best pledge-generating first-run program in public television history had raised about $12.5 million.

The *Doo Wop* music concert, in its first run, raised twice that: $26 million. So public stations ran it again a few months later, and Lubinsky told me the total reached some $50 million.

And it has continued and grown into additional spin-off concerts that have raised a *fortune* in pledges for public television.

All because television decided, for once, to simply *acknowledge* and *celebrate* the lives of an overlooked and underappreciated generation.

And Silents responded by reaching for their phones and delivering record-breaking donations.

Again, these are just a few examples of the many industries that are – or should be – cashing in on the wealthy, free-spending, non-brand-loyal Silent Generation.

Silents: Their future

I have the privilege to present Generational Strategy to live audiences in every corner of the country. But after each presentation, I then get to *learn*, during the question-and-answer session that follows. I've absorbed Americans' comments about our generations. And here's the "hope" that constantly surfaces when all generations discuss the Silents.

Silents, you carry something very special inside of you. You carry a memory that younger generations don't carry, which will become clear when you read the chapters about Gen X and Millennials.

Along with the G.I.s and primarily the First-Wave Boomers, you carry a first-person, direct-experience knowledge of an America that was fulfilling its promise as you came of age.

An America that took on big problems and *solved* them. An America in which neighbors helped neighbors. An America in which bosses and subordinates were on the same side. An America in which the family unit was solid and kids grew up feeling loved and safe and guided. An America whose radio and television and music industries brought out our best instincts instead of our worst. An America whose citizens were unrushed enough to practice common courtesy with each other. An America that knew how to smile. And laugh. An America that dared to dream big dreams and was idealistic and sassy enough to think – to *know* – it could realize them. An America that truly believed it could achieve perfection.

It is an America that Gen Xers and Millennials – this is difficult to comprehend, isn't it? – have not experienced in nearly the same full glory as you did. Your kids and grandkids don't know how magnificent everyday American life can be. Their only knowledge of America is best described by a woman who has spent her career working for our government's child services agencies for many years. "For the past thirty years," she recently told me, describing the disappointment of American citizens with their nation's leaders, "it feels like we Americans have been suffering from a *low-grade flu.*"

Can you Silents somehow find a way – and will they give you the time, in their busy lives – to impart the story of the America that can be, the America that *you know*, to your skeptical children and grandchildren so they, too, will demand that their country not rest until it's achieved the ideal, rather than shrug their shoulders and simply accept this low-grade flu that most of them assume is the American *norm?*

If you can find a way to convey the America *you* know to the younger generations, it might become your generation's greatest legacy.

Chapter 3

Marketing To Silents
Tips, tactics, and guidelines

In this book, each generation's section concludes with two chapters to help businesspeople to deal with that generation in the (1) marketplace and (2) workplace. These next two chapters are designed to be quick-find reference manuals that you can use in the months and years to come to speedily refresh your memory of the Silent Generation and review specific tips and tactics to effectively "connect" with them.

REMEMBER:

Silents have more spending power than any prior generation to reach their current age bracket and life stage.

However, many Silent blacks and single women are not in the same solid financial position as that of many white couples and white men, because they faced job and wage discrimination during many of their career years.

Silents feel that being open to new products and services helps them to think and live *young*, which is a key motivator to this generation. This means they are receptive to advertising, to changing brands, and to trying new products.

They are a thoughtful, patriotic, politically active, news-reading, plugged-in, smart generation.

Many will work, at least part-time, in retirement. And many will do so not because they need the money but instead to stay active, involved, and "alive."

They spend freely on a long list of categories, such as their grandchildren, travel, automobiles, housing, real estate, financial services, health care, dining, autos, and many others. They've worked diligently in their careers and feel they've now *earned the right* to reward themselves.

Not only that, many of them have a vague sense of having lived conforming lives that were "safe, apolitical, and boring – but now it's our turn!'" They have a pent-up desire to grab life for all they can, and many possess the spending power to act on that urge.

Silents are a charitable generation.

Don't forget their passion to connect with their grandchildren. They can recall the solidarity of the American family from their own childhood era, they've witnessed its deterioration over the past several decades, and they now want to do all they can to restrengthen the family unit by being a constant and positive presence in the lives of their kids and grandkids. Because so many of their children are time-stressed and/or divorced or single parents, a growing number of Silents are involved in the *primary* care of those grandkids and, as such, are involved in the purchases of products and services associated with such care.

When I was presenting this information at a Midwest business conference in Indianapolis and showed a Walt Disney World commercial showing Silent grandparents and their grandson vacationing together without the boys' parents, a Silent male in the audience smiled and raised his hand. "Amazing", he said. "At this very moment, my wife and our grandchildren are at Disney World together, giving our busy Gen X children a chance to have some time for themselves."

Here are tips, tactics, and guidelines for marketing, advertising, communicating, and messaging to an important generation in the American marketplace:

TIPS, TACTICS, GUIDELINES –
MARKETING TO THE SILENTS

Many of them don't know they're called the Silent Generation, and some who do don't like the label. But when you explain the name's history, they get it and accept it.

They grew up *before malls,* when local store owners and clerks knew their names, knew their families, and stood behind their products in a one-to-one way. So give them genuinely personal service. To many Silents (and Boomers, for that matter, who also remember *pre-mall*), current-day customer service is impersonal and often downright horrible. That means *opportunity* for the vendor who delivers it to Silents' high standards. Develop a relationship with them. Get to know them. Talk with them.

Courtesy is very important to Silents.

It's okay to be a bit more formal when messaging to this generation. Silents came of age with a strong emphasis on manners and politeness and so are receptive to it. "Please," "Thank you," "Sir," and "Ma'am" are appreciated. So are prompt and full responses to their questions. This, by the way, also happens to work with *all* generations.

Does your marketing and advertising and customer service staff include members of the Silent Generation? If not, is there someone on your staff whom you trust to truly understand them? If not, might it be a good idea to hire a Silent, or Silents, even if on a part-time or consulting basis? Or conduct Silent-specific research?

Are you planning on giving a Silent client or prospective client your business card? If so, what type size and color contrast are you using on your card? Is it Silent friendly or has your graphic artist decided to express his or her creative side with a cute look but a small-type, low-color-contrast, user-unfriendly, difficult-to-read card? Is your staff top-heavy with younger employees who aren't sensitized to sight diminution that increases as we age? A young graphic artist designed my company's first batch of business cards. Beautiful cards. Impossible to read. I redesigned the second batch myself to be reader friendly instead of simply another pretty addition to the artist's own portfolio.

Use multigenerational images and audio in your marketing to them. Silents and their children. Silents and their grandkids.

Nostalgia and sentimentality work: these emotions connect Silents to their comfortable past; plus, Silents feel overlooked and underappreciated, and the use of nostalgic references from their youth *acknowledges* them.

Bargains and discounts and coupons and premiums work. Silents grew up with green stamps, yellow stamps, and plaid stamps. They also remember receiving a free water glass for each fill-up at the "service station." Fun memories and savings. Silents love both. The Great Depression and World War II give this generation a special respect for the value of a dollar that younger generations don't possess.

Celebrate Silents' maturity and wisdom and experience with your message; *they've come a long way, baby.*

Demonstrate how your product or service gives Silents the opportunity for first-time experiences and personal growth. But wrap these first-time experiences in security and safety, not high-risk uncertainty. Soften the idea of "new" and punch-up the idea of "enhance your life."

Don't hype. Don't lie. Prove your claim. Over the years, this generation has been pitched a gazillion versions of "new-and-improved" laundry detergents but have seldom seen their *whites get whiter.* They've been disappointed many times.

Don't rush your story, but don't dawdle either. Silents have the time – and will take the time – to read your message. Silents are avid consumers of printed text.

Use their life passages to connect with them. Grandparenthood. Retirement and free time. Moving. Career or hobby change. Loss of spouse. Volunteerism. Philanthropy. Eldercare. Grandchild care. And so on.

The "grand slam" in generational marketing strategy occurs when a generation brings its unique core values to a new life passage. *At that intersection of generational values and new life passage stands a huge opportunity for marketers.*

Various types of loyalty/incentive programs can work with Silents.

Let them interact. They want to be experiential. Nabisco introduced Eggbeaters by cooking more than 300,000 breakfasts in more than 1,800 senior centers nationwide; participating seniors received a recipe book and coupons. Excellent.

Group events with other Silents can be especially effective. Don't give Silents a tutorial CD Rom explaining your product and ask them to sit alone and learn about it on the computer. This is a "people" generation.

Educate. Educate. Educate. Silents are hungry to learn.

Sell the *benefits* to Silents of your product or service but also its *features*. Silents came of age when advertising did focus upon features more than brand or emotion. So don't overlook features. Find an old television commercial when actress Betty Furness demonstrated the features of a 1950s' refrigerator.

The purchase must be easy and hassle free to make.

Make it memorable by keeping it simple. Age tends to diminish short-term and verbal memory. Visual images – especially photographs – are effective. Messages should be simple and explicit and carefully paced. Think of MTV's apparent creative philosophy of four images per second, and then do the exact opposite.

Use Silent Generation grandparents, and their values, to reach their grandkids. For example, let Grandma and Grandpa open up a passbook savings account at the bank for their grandchildren, and reward Grandma and Grandpa for doing so with special gifts and promotions. Wendy's, Disney World, Energizer, and others have created advertising messages in which the on-camera talent is Silent grandparent and Xer or Millennial grandchild.

Silents don't especially want to be "singled out." Connect them with other generations.

Which media work with Silents?

- Print. Silents devour the daily paper and understand it is the most trustworthy source of objective, comprehensive, and factual coverage of daily life. Silents want the best obtainable version of the truth, not the blowhard opinions of radio talk shows, cable TV's noise-making half hours, and Internet blogs. Newspapers – and the weekly news magazines like *Time, Newsweek,*

U.S. News and World Report, Newsweek, and a few others – have earned the Silents' trust over the decades.

- Television. Don't overlook the possibility of under-writing local or national *public* television shows. In an ocean of advertising clutter on commercial media these days, public television remains an island of non-clutter.

- Direct-Response TV. Longer-form messages are a good fit for Silents' time availability and their desire and need to hear and digest the entire story. Long-form also permits you to prove your claim.

- Direct Mail. You can tell your story more complete-ly, and they have time to read it. And direct mail can remain in front of them on the coffee table, unlike here-and-gone broadcast messages. So direct mail is comfortable and enables Silents to recheck the de-tails. But eliminate the hype and don't hide the bad news (cost, interest rate, etc.) deep in the bowels of your message.

- Women's Magazines. These magazines were immense-ly important and influential during the Silents' for-mative years because television didn't yet dominate the living room. Check the most recent research at any given time on which specific titles are hot, but generally speaking, the fashion and home and travel magazines that target mature women have performed quite well.

- Telemarketing. In the 1990s and early 2000s, telemar-keting earned such a wretched reputation for intrusion and scamming that, still true today, it hasn't recovered and might never. Silents know unethical hustlers target older consumers and use telemarketing to confuse them and seduce them into a quick phone-buy. And most Silents - and G.I.s - have a very negative response to telemarketing, even if the call comes from an existing vendor, such as their own bank or auto dealer. However, some telemarketing is succeeding.

- Internet. The percentage of Silents who are online is escalating daily – and notably. Because the Internet landscape is going to be in constant flux for some years to come, you'll need to find the latest research as to *how* Silents are using it and which Web sites they most frequently visit, but most research studies to date indicate that Silents use the Internet to:

  - send e-mail to family and friends.
  - monitor news events and weather.
  - research health information.
  - make purchases online from trusted merchants.
  - research other topics.
  - research products/services to purchase offline.
  - research stocks and investments; online banking.
  - play games.
  - conduct genealogy research.
  - access discussions.

Silents and G.I.s view the Internet primarily as a way to keep in touch with family members and friends. Boomers view it as an electronic encyclopedia and a source of information, although they're using it more often now

for entertainment. Xers view it as information *and* enter-tainment. Millennials view it as information, entertain-ment, and the air they breathe, as another appendage to their bodies.

Silents might have difficulty with complex Web sites. So make it straightforward, and use *text* cues to guide them through the sites. But don't load up your pages with too much text. Also, can you give them a one-click method to increase text size? Use color-coding and other tech-niques to make it simple to use. Reduce your clutter.

Examine your own marketing/advertising/product de-velopment personnel and attitudes.

- Look in the mirror: are your organization's decision makers younger than Silents and susceptible to stereo-typing? Is there a good reason you don't have Silents on your staff?

- Remember the current times: there is a profound shift in the American marketplace in the direction of the fifty-plus generations and demos. Do you need to erase some old tapes playing in your head?

Kevin O'Keefe, managing director of Weber Shandwick, a PR firm with clients that target Silents, told Ad Age mag-azine, "Clearly, marketers will have to reorient forty years of thinking. Marketers fall into old patterns and bad as-sumptions even as they realize how critical this group is."

Age seventy is the new fifty. Age eighty is the new sixty. Not just a cute phrase. True. Ignore this generation at your own risk.

The Silents have made enormous contributions to history, but they've never been applauded. First marketer/advertiser to publicly applaud them wins.

They are worthy of media coverage, but they don't receive it. Cover them, and win.

They are worthy of celebration, but they don't know it. Celebrate them, and win.

They are a unified generation with distinctive values and attitudes, but many of them don't think of their age cohort as a generation. In this regard, they're like Xers and unlike G.I.s and Boomers and Millennials. So, teach them about their own generation, and you'll have their attention.

Don't patronize or offend them with your message. Silents are not sweet little old ladies and men.

Silents, whose core values are rooted in the pragmatism of the depression and war, respond to *rational* appeals.

Repetition of message helps.

Emotional hot buttons: their generation's legacy; its contribution; security; independence; shared experiences with their children and great grandchildren; long and healthy lives.

Older consumers prefer older sales and customer service personnel. (And so do a lot of younger consumers)!

They also desire point-of-sale and point-of-purchase user friendliness in the stores. Are your POP and POS signage Silent friendly?

Chapter 4

Silents In The Workplace
Tips, tactics, and guidelines

A recent study documents that older workers are usually better than younger ones at problem solving but sometimes need more time than younger workers to learn complex new tasks.

Now, with their unique formative years, and with the unique generational core values and attitudes that were molded in those formative years, who are these people in the workplace???

Home Depot and AARP
"This is a gold mine of resources for us."

In what *The Wall Street Journal* described as the first-ever attempt to target thousands of mostly Silent workers, Home Depot and AARP recently launched a national hiring partnership.

AARP is recruiting and training Silent workers (and the

very leading edge of Boomers), and Home Depot will hire them in all departments.

Robert Nardelli, then chairman of Home Depot, said this in an interview:

"When you look at the skill set, the knowledge and career experience, and the passion of these members of AARP, this is a gold mine of resources for us to draw upon."

The Silent Generation will be working energetically for many years, and they bring a unique set of core values and attitudes, skills, and wisdom to the workplace that other generations don't possess and will thus welcome the opportunity to learn.

Consider the title of a recent *BusinessWeek* cover story: "Old. Smart. Productive." This story reminds us, "High-level work is getting easier for the old. Internet search engines serve as auxiliary memories (and) compensate for loss of memory." And they're creative, drawing upon a lifetime of observation and experimentation.

Urban Institute senior fellow C. Eugene Steurerle said this when he addressed the House Ways and Means Committee in 2005: "People in their late fifties, sixties, and seventies have now become the largest underutilized pool of human resources in the economy."

Silents at Work

- They're disciplined.
- Courteous and diplomatic.*

- Good manners are important to them.
- Strong work ethic.
- More private than younger workers.**

* The president of a regional bank in the Pacific Northwest attended one of my recent workshops in Oregon and shared this with me afterward: He explained that the employees who interact most often with bank customers are the tellers, and *teller* is an entry-level position. His bank was finding that younger generations of tellers are less attentive and less courteous with its customers than older generations had been at that same age. And tellers, he emphasized, represent the "face," the personality of a bank. If Silents want to remain active and vital, it might be a good strategy for banks to hire Silents – maybe even retired ones who want to work only part-time – to be their tellers.

** In conversations with co-workers, Silents are probably much less likely than Xers and Millennials to share the intimacies of their personal lives. Silents did not come of age with the daytime sleaze talk shows. Xers and Millennials did, when everyday people have gleefully shared their most intimate – and often disgusting – secrets on national television. Younger generations: be aware of this generational difference and be sensitive to it when conversing with Silents and G.I.s and yes, even Boomers.

- Loyal/less attrition.
- Respect for authority and company history.
- Team players.
- Consensus builders.*

* One of the reasons Silents have distinguished themselves in the so-called helping professions is their core value of inclusiveness. If ten employees are seated around the conference table and the discussion is led by a Silent, you can be fairly certain all ten will have a generous opportunity to be heard.

- Might be more flexible than younger generations on hours (fewer family entanglements).
- Fountain of wisdom. Think of all they've seen in their lives and careers.
- Valuable mentors to younger generations.
- The company comes first.
- Stick to it.
- Don't rock the boat.
- Especially good social and interpersonal skills; deal well with customers and clients.*
- Good "front" people for an organization; seldom make politically incorrect blunder.
- Energetic and productive and smart.

* Would some of your clients and customers *prefer* to deal with Silents rather than younger employees?

Recruiting Silents

- Identify and eliminate obsolete thinking and age bias in your HR and management culture.
- Identify the best message channels to reach this generation of new prospects.
- Review the copy for your job recruitment ads; is it tilted toward younger employees, with words like "eager"

and "energetic," or does it emphasize "experience" and "maturity"?

- Be creative and flexible with compensation, retirement, pension, and benefit plans.
- Explain the company's history. They'll care. They'll be genuinely interested.
- Explain the organization's big picture and goals and processes.
- Don't be guilty of Buzzword Bias.*

* From a corporate client of mine comes this alert. He told me his organization had screwed up. His Human Resource people had discovered that, in their recruitment and screening of candidates, they had fallen victim to Buzzword Bias. As he explains it, the organization was developing, as most organizations do, a bunch of new workplace buzzwords. The latest hip, trendy shorthand du jour. These buzzwords aren't especially important, he added, but recruiters had been evaluating candidates partially on whether the candidates were familiar with them. Younger candidates tended to know the buzzwords, older candidates often didn't. And the recruiters finally realized they had allowed some talented older candidates to slip right through their fingers, and for the stupidest of reasons. So, put your entire recruitment process under the microscope. Are you guilty of needless Buzzword Bias in your recruitment ads, resumé review, candidate screening, interviewing, evaluation, and final selection?

Managing Silents

- Train Silents–especially management–in Generational Workforce Diversity.*

- Identify, respect, and use their generation's unique strengths.
- Might need technology training. Let people train them, not a CD Rom.
- Give them personal attention.
- Don't mistake silence and courtesy for disinterest.**

* Silents began their career years when the American workplace was a very different culture from what it is today. Teach them why the workplace values and attitudes of Boomers, Xers, and Millennials are often not the same as their own, and teach them how to understand and work harmoniously with the other generations.

** In a group meeting, their silence and calmness and unwillingness to interrupt others and talk loudly to make their point is a result of Silents' core values of courtesy and inclusiveness. Silents usually listen – and think – before they talk. They're less aggressive in conversation than Boomers might be, *but they're fully engaged.*

- Be sensitive to their age.*
- Consider new work arrangements: phased retirement; creative compensation and benefit and pension plans; job sharing and leave sharing; part-time, flextime, telecommuting; and more.**
- Use their teaching and mentoring skills.***
- Use their wisdom and experience.

* This tip actually covers multiple generations. Is your workplace lighting adequate, right down to the individual workstation? Are your chairs comfortable for all ages? Floors solid and even? In lengthy meetings, are you scheduling frequent-enough restroom breaks? What time of day are you scheduling those meetings? What about extraneous noise? (One of my clients, an audiology retailer, says some 20,000,000 Americans – including increasing numbers of Gen Xers, who grew up with stereo headsets that slammed music into their eardrums from point-blank range – have such significant hearing loss they *should* be wearing hearing aids, but aren't. *20,000,000.*)

** After lopping off higher-paid older workers in favor of cheaper and younger ones for years, American business now recognizes *it must do everything it can to retain the workplace values and wisdom of Silents and Boomers. Age discrimination in the workplace is dying a very swift death.* So we're just now entering a golden era of creative workplace accommodations: part-time, flextime, telecommuting, job sharing, leave sharing, generationally customized compensation and benefit plans, and accommodations for personal-life issues. Is your organization thinking outside the box to embrace Silents (and Boomers)? An insurance agency client of mine has rehired a retired Silent to work part-time as its accountant. The Silent was the perfect candidate, didn't need the work or the money but enjoyed working, and so the deal was this: "I'll work for you if it won't disrupt my Wednesday round of golf with my friends." Done! The boss says the Silent's wisdom and experience are irreplaceable and the work always gets done accurately and on time (Natch! He's a Silent). And the weekly golf outing is preserved.

*** As a generation, the Silents have distinguished themselves in the helping professions. Many of them are expert at *teaching.* Harness that generational skill. However, teaching is one thing. Mentoring is another. Mentoring programs, at the moment, are sometimes succeeding and sometimes failing. But Silents have skills that younger generations don't possess. And don't forget two-way mentoring, because younger generations have skills Silents don't possess.

Chapter 5

The Boomers
It's Their Turn At The Top

FORMATIVE YEARS, CORE VALUES,
ADULTHOOD, FUTURE

Now, let's move to that generation that, as Silent Frank Kaiser wrote, "squeezes life for all of its satisfactions."

August 1945.

World War II ends, the last of sixteen million young, triumphant, virile, and apparently quite horny American soldiers come home all at once, step off the train in their hometowns all at once, get married all at once, jump in the sack with their beloved brides all at once...

... and nine months later, the historic American Baby Boom is *on*. And it will continue for nineteen years.

They were *really* horny.

Born: 1946 to 1964
79,907,844 born
Formative years: '50s, '60s, '70s

The nineteen birth years of the older Silent Generation had produced fewer than forty-seven million babies.

The nineteen years of the Boom are about to create nearly 80,000,000 Mouseketeers.

And this generation's formative years will be, primarily, the 1950s, '60s, '70s, and early '80s.

Each generation has what is called a First Wave and a Second Wave. Older half and younger half. Typically, the two waves are slightly different in their values but still share enough core values to be a single generation. And that's absolutely true with Boomers, only their differences are a little more pronounced.

The First-Wave Boomers were born from 1946 to 1954. Second-Wave'ers: from 1955 to 1964.

Dr. Spock

As the First-Wave Boomer babies are arriving, their mostly G.I.-Generation mothers are faithfully administering the parental wisdom of a pediatrician named Dr. Benjamin Spock, who, in *The Common Sense Book of Baby and Child Care,* which comes out in 1946 and will ultimately sell some fifty million copies, writes four words that will help to change the course of American history:

"We need idealistic children."

Dr. Spock, be careful what you ask for. You just might get it.

First-Wave Boomer kids are raised by stay-at-home mothers who consider themselves democratic and tolerant. Their fathers become the rock-solid *provider* figures in their lives.

And these children come of age embracing the idealism that their parents and educators are preaching and teaching every day, in the living room and the classroom.

They're also imbued, by their elders, with another strong message: a message of what is *right* and what is *wrong*, what is good and what is bad, what you do and what you don't do. As Boomers come of age, there isn't much gray area – not much room for *negotiating* with Mom and Dad – when it comes to right and wrong.

And in the 1960s, after spending their early childhood in the carefree and innocent Happy Days of the '50s, that cocktail – that recipe of idealism and a strong sense of right and wrong – goes a long way in explaining one of the most tumultuous periods, but also one of the most socially enlightening periods, in our nation's history...

The Consciousness Movement
1961 to 1975

...the so-called Consciousness Movement of 1961 to 1975, but which most of us refer to as simply the Sixties.

As one magazine writer would describe it many years later, this is the period when America *"remakes itself in fairer terms, beginning the process of righting our wrongs."* (I read that powerful line at 40,000 feet, on a flight to the west coast, but I failed to rip the article from the airline magazine and so regrettably don't have the author's name. Whoever you are, thank you for capturing the Consciousness Movement so eloquently.)

Their parents had battled an economic depression and then military enemies in their younger years.

As the First-Wave Boomers come of age, and as they sit across the dinner table each night from this generation of engaged, empowered, visionary, nothing-is-impossible parents, they feel the same sense of purpose and activism, only now it's against different enemies.

And during this fifteen-year convulsion in America, First-Wave Boomers deliver their passion, their idealism, and their masses to no fewer than six major cultural revolutions, most considered very noble and selfless, but some considered very damaging and selfish.

By the way, the Boomers provided the passion and idealism and masses, but the individual *leaders* arc mostly Silents, with a couple of G.I.s. Take a look:

1. Civil Rights Movement	King, Malcolm X, Chavez, Means
2. Feminist Movement	Gloria Steinem
3. Ecology Movement	six of first seven EPA Chiefs
4. War Protest Movement	Chicago Seven, SDS, and others

5. Sexual Revolution   Hugh Hefner
6. Drug Revolution   Timothy Leary

The civil rights movement of the '60s is led by Silent Generation members Martin Luther King, Jr. and Malcolm X for African-Americans; by Silent Cesar Chavez for Mexican-Americans; and by Silent Russell Means for AIM, the American Indian Movement.

The icon of the feminist movement is Gloria Steinem, a Silent.

The ecology movement begins during the Consciousness Movement and six of the first seven directors of the newly created Environmental Protection Agency are Silents.

The war protest movement is spearheaded by The Chicago Seven, Students for a Democratic Society, and many other local and national groups, led primarily by Silents.

The sexual revolution: Playboy magazine founder Hugh Hefner. He's born in mid-1926, right on the "cusp" between Silents and G.I.s.

And the crusader for the drug revolution is G.I. Generation member Dr. Timothy Leary, who coins the phrase, "*turn on, tune in, drop out.*"

'Nam

The war in Vietnam profoundly affects all Boomers, but especially the First-Wave'ers.

More than three million soldiers serve in Southeast Asia during the war. More than 58,000 die. The average age of the American soldier fighting there is nineteen.

Three lifelong Boomer core values will emerge from the war their generation of soldiers will always refer to in shorthand, as simply 'Nam.

One and Two: a Boomer sense of *empowerment* and *engagement*. Protests and pressure by American citizens of many ages, but primarily by young Boomers, influence the U.S. government's decision to ultimately quit the war. From that comes a Boomer value of *empowerment*, the belief that the masses can influence their government, that America really is a government of, for, and by the people. And with that empowerment comes the companion core value of *engagement*: *I believe I can influence the outcome, so I'm going to engage in the democratic process.*

Three: for a number of Boomers and some younger Silents, this will be a hard-learned lesson. But years later, the generational core value will be unambiguous, and younger generations will learn from what many Boomers consider a mistake during 'Nam, when protesting Boomers *criticize American soldiers for their participation in the war.* The revised core value that emerged years after 'Nam is this: *we can – and should – vigorously criticize our government if we believe its decisions about military combat are incorrect, but we will never – never again – fail to support our troops.*

"I have a dream today!"

For African-Americans, this is it!

The modern civil rights movement – the Glorious Struggle – now reaches full bloom and becomes an emotional roller-coaster ride of historic joy and historic anguish, especially for the black Boomers who are in their all-important formative years.

Here's just a very small sample of what Boomer blacks and whites – who are trying so hard to extend the hand of friendship to each other – witness as their generation comes of age:

1963: Dr. King's historic I Have A Dream speech.
1964: Passage of historic civil rights legislation
       by Congress.
1965: The assassination of Malcolm X.
1966: The founding of the Black Panther Party.
1967: The worst urban riots in U.S. history.
1968: The assassinations of Dr. King and Bobby Kennedy.

Throughout their formative years, Boomer blacks will see their brothers and sisters and, in some cases, their mothers and fathers make tremendous progress in American life, especially in the American workplace.

Keep this in mind: First-Wave Boomers have always been one of the more scrutinized and judged age cohorts.

They were in kindergarten and elementary and junior-high school in the Happy Days of the '50s and very early '60s. And when they had looked upward to those older, cooler Silent Generation high schoolers and college students, they saw joy, innocence, and carefree good times, and they fully expected their own teenage and early-adult years would be just like that.

To this day, most First-Wave Boomers still can't fully explain how and why it erupted as it did during the Consciousness Movement.

A pop culture professor at Ohio State University thinks it was actor Dennis Hopper who first uttered the famous line about the Consciousness Movement: "Anyone who tells you he *recalls the '60s clearly*... probably wasn't there."

And the book *Generations: The History of America's Future 1584 to 2069* shares the comment of a senior student at Radcliffe College, who in her 1968 commencement speech says it a bit more seriously for her fellow First-Wave Boomers:

"We do not feel like a cool, swinging generation. We are eaten up by an intensity that we cannot name."

What they learned during their formative years was idealism and that strong sense of right and wrong.

In the '60s, First-Wave Boomers react to what they're witnessing all around them in perhaps the only way a generation raised on those core values *can* react.

Now then, after launching all of these cultural revolutions, the inevitable occurs. The First-Wave Boomers must leave school, enter adulthood, launch their careers, and start their families. They will now disappear from the front pages of the nation's newspapers for a quarter century.

Behind them come the Second-Wave Boomers:

Second-Wave Boomers
Born: 1955 to 1964
Graduate H.S. late '70s to early '80s

Born from 1955 to 1964, these are the folks who graduate from high school from the mid '70s to the very early '80s.

Missed the social protests
Don't feel like Boomers or Xers
Who are we?

Many of them haven't *felt* like Boomers, primarily because the word "Boomer" is so strongly associated with the social activism that is ending just as they're becoming old enough to join it. So Second-Wave Boomers, who come of age with the same sense of empowerment and engagement as First-Wave'ers, generally don't march in the streets, burn their bras for peace, or get tear-gassed.

But they also know this: they don't feel like those younger Gen Xers either.

And to this day, they've never had the question answered, *who are we?* So we'll see if we can help them.

Nuclear families intact
Live life to the fullest
Unlimited possibilities
Career driven

Like First-Wave Boomers, most Second-Wave'ers grow up with their nuclear families intact – not much divorce amongst their parents. And this alone molds a long list of core values similar to the older Boomers and dissimilar from Gen X.

They also come of age when anything seems possible in this marvelous country called America.

Boomers, to their good fortune, come of age during perhaps the most ideal period in American history to be a kid. *America can do anything!* Land a man on the moon, make historic progress against our own worst prejudices, cure disease, enjoy strong family life and stable work life and safe neighborhoods. *Wow!*

The TV sitcom *The Wonder Years,* which is all about being a Boomer kid back then, opens each episode with 5 words that capture the era: "a golden age for kids".

Second-Wave Boomers move through their formative years feeling hope and opportunity all around them. And so they share the same powerful go-for-it-in-life, live-life-to-the-fullest mindset as their older Boomer brothers and sisters.

What's more, the American economy is rolling during *most* of their formative years, so Second-Wave'ers also think America is going to offer them unlimited career and income possibilities.

From all of this, they grow up feeling a strong sense of nation and patriotism. And they're career driven, willing to work long hours and be loyal to the company.

Belief in meritocracy
Individuality
Merging of black-white cultures
Forever-young mentality

They are also very-much-Boomer in their belief in meritocracy, the belief that you advance in your career by way of hard, smart, and honest work. Not by shortcuts or backstabbing.

To both waves of this generation, individuality means personal growth.

This is also when black Boomers, propelled by the Civil Rights Movement and the black pride movement that comes with it, begin to see their white Boomer brothers and sisters embracing their African-American culture for the first time: all of a sudden, music, movies, TV, fashion, slang, and other important youth touchstones are now crossing over *in both directions.*

By contrast, in the '50s when *Silent* kids were in their teens, some black entertainers often had their hair straightened so as to be more appealing to white audiences. But now, some white Boomer kids are trying to grow their own curly "Afros."

And from this comes a core value in *all* Boomers of taking pride in reducing the black-white gap in America.

And finally, these Second-Wave Boomers are true Boomers in one other very important core value. They think young, without even knowing it, and without trying. A forever-young mentality.

So that's how Second-Wave'ers are very much Boomer. Here's how they're somewhat different.

In the '70s, Second-Wave Boomers are still in the final part of their formative years. And this is when it begins to unravel a bit in America: Watergate, a higher cost of living, more limited career opportunities, job layoffs, and more cynical and vulgar commercial radio, television, and music industries.

Skeptical, not cynical
More money motivated
Less optimistic

And so these Second-Wave Boomers also develop some core values slightly different from the First Wave. They become a bit more skeptical about just how idealistic America really is, but not hard-bitten cynical like younger Gen Xers will understandably become in another decade.

Also, they become more motivated by money, as America enters the *Decade of Greed,* as the late '70s and '80s are remembered, a very materialistic and acquisitive time in America.

Finally, Second-Wave Boomers become a bit less optimistic about how unlimited the career opportunity in this country really is going to be for them when they enter adulthood.

But big picture – and unmistakably – Second-Wave Boomers are card-carrying members of the Baby Boom Generation. The core values they possess are overwhelmingly Boomer.

By the way, Second-Wave'ers know how to party hardy! In the immediate aftermath of the fifteen-year-long struggle of the Consciousness Movement, America in the '70s and '80s needs to take a deep breath and have some fun. Second-Wave'ers are ready, willing, and able. Do all of you Second-Wave'ers *clearly remember* the '70s and early '80s?

Didn't think so.

Struggle with marriage and parenthood

In adulthood, Boomers as a generation struggle terribly with marriage. They – along with a number of younger Silents – send the divorce rate over the moon, for a variety of reasons.

Untold hundreds of thousands of them "have to get married" as the sexual revolution arrives in their schools and communities before many of the girls can gain access to the birth control pill. And during this time in the '60s and very early '70s, abortion is not yet a legal option and seldom a moral option for this generation. So many are "forced" into marriages with sexual partners rather than with chosen lifelong companions, and many are simply too young and immature to handle these *shotgun marriages,* many of which swiftly collapse, trapping their GenX children in a bewilderment and frustration that is chronicled in that generation's upcoming chapters.

And marriage is frequently difficult even for those Boomers who don't get pregnant and who do marry with all of the traditional good intentions, because the only model of marriage this generation has ever known – the one they witnessed in their parents and grandparents – disappears, as the women's movement suddenly opens career doors for women and the birth control pill gives them nearly complete control over their reproduction. With many Boomer women financially independent and as career driven as they are family driven, they do not feel compelled to remain in unsatisfactory marriages. And this is a generation that also pursues the absolute ideal in life. A perfectionist mindset. If marriage doesn't meet their high standards, dispose of it.

In addition, the sexual freedom mentality just created by the invention of the pill is also increasing marital infidelity and, with it, still more divorce.

And in 1971, according to Census Bureau data, the divorce rate in the United States is an astonishing 165 percent higher than it had been only ten years earlier.

Singer-songwriter Carole King, as she has done so often in her acclaimed career, captures – with collaborator Toni Stern – this divorce epidemic with her powerful, Grammy-winning 1971 song, "It's Too Late":

"Stayed in bed all morning just to pass the time...
There's something wrong and there can be no denying...

One of us is changing, or maybe we just stopped trying.
And it's too late, baby, now it's too late,
Though we really did try to make it.
Something inside has died...
And I can't hide and I just can't fake it...."

Boomers also will struggle with parenting, and these difficulties will also be presented in the chapters covering their Gen X children.

American life is changing so swiftly now!

And the American family unit is undergoing seismic transformation from what Boomers had known in their own childhood.

They *want* to be perfect in their parenting and careers, but there's no manual to tell them how to balance the two in this new model. Boomers thus become the generation that must *write* that manual. They must conduct the trial *and error* to find out what will and won't work.

Excel in the workplace
Continue the fight

But if they struggle with marriage and parenting, Boomers will be nothing short of brilliant in the American workplace. And they will continue their generation's sincere crusade for a more ethical, more ideal America.

Ambushed
Fierce competition
Great expectations

The Silent Generation white men, remember, have enjoyed that uncommonly smooth career passage.

The Boomers, conversely, will forever be the ambushed generation, because they enter the work world expecting their careers to proceed as nicely as the generation right ahead of them, but then get bushwhacked in early- to mid-career with a spate of corporate down-sizing, right-sizing, reengineering, consolidation, outsourcing, off-shoring, age discrimination, and the executive-corruption and executive-greed meltdown of their older bosses, all on a colossal scale.

Not only are they ambushed by the cutbacks and corruption, but Boomers also are so massive in number that they will face fierce, lifelong competition *from their fellow Boomers* for the same jobs and promotions. The Silent Generation, and younger Gen X, both so few in numbers, will never suffer from that same imbalance of worker supply and demand.

Not only are Boomers so much more numerous but also, with their arrival in adulthood, the competition for jobs and promotions is no longer restricted to white males, as it had been with prior generations.

Now the competition also comes from women and blacks, two subsets of Boomers who are astonished by the hard-earned opportunities *finally* being extended to them, but who also feel extraordinary pressure to perform *perfectly*.

There's one other stress-builder for Boomers that few of them probably even recognize: they had been told or had simply sensed, from an early age, that they are a *special generation* who came along at a *special time* in American history, and that special achievement would always be expected from them. And this generation does not want to disappoint. Boomers know the enormous struggle and sacrifice by their parents' and their grandparents' generations. They know they've been given uncommon opportunity, and they want desperately to deliver. Remember that Radcliffe College quote from 1968: "We are eaten up by an intensity that we cannot name."

So with those generational core values, which came from their unique formative years, Boomers enter adulthood as career-driven workaholics. This is the generation that defines itself by its work – by its contribution – and *always will.*

Boomers make long-hour workweeks the norm. They take work home. Work on weekends. They willingly accept job transfers to other cities and states and nations. They've been described as the generation that lives the motto, T-G-I-M.

Thank God It's Monday.

Layoffs
Age discrimination
Eldercare/childcare

But layoffs begin hitting many Boomers in mid- or even early-career, and now today they also face illegal –

although rapidly disappearing – age discrimination as some of them search for new jobs and careers.

Not only that, Boomers are feeling the bookend pressures of both eldercare, as their beloved parents live longer than parents have ever lived, and childcare, as many of their twenty-something kids remain at home longer.

At this moment, and through the year 2014, Boomers will be turning age fifty at the rate of about one Boomer *every seven seconds*, or more than 370,000 every month. Their aging, coupled with the fact that all of us are living longer, is about to have an incomprehensible impact on our nation.

With the aging of the Boomers, such issues as longer and more flexible careers, Social Security, pension plans, health, housing, eldercare, politics, financial security, philanthropy, volunteerism, and the American marketplace, workplace, and lifestyle are about to undergo staggering transformation.

No hurry to retire

And about retiring? This is the generation – the men and the women – who, in unprecedented numbers, won't.

Boomers define themselves by their work.

Rewriting *The Book of Life*

Boomers have rewritten that good ol' *Book of Life* every

day of their lives. They've done so many things so differently from the ways they had been done before.

And to the other generations who had assumed – and in many cases, hoped – that Boomers would one day slow down, become a bit more conservative, and go gently into their next life passage...

guess again.

As First Wave'ers become empty nesters, with Second Wave'ers soon to follow, and as their careers strike at least a more reasonable balance, their activism – their sense of right and wrong – is beginning to reemerge. They see an America that isn't fulfilling its promise. And that is unacceptable.

The Boomers aren't done.

They're getting active again on causes. And this activism is gaining momentum. The Boomer masses are discovering that the Internet can be the same gathering place today that the college campus was in the '60s.

One powerhouse example is moveon.org, a political action organization based in the San Francisco Bay Area, founded by a couple of Boomers and Xers. It has raised astronomical sums in order to support candidates and ballot issues.

Another example: according to a recent news report, Peace Corps volunteerism by age fifty-plus is higher than ever.

When we think of Boomer empowerment and engagement, we tend to think back to the mass protests of the sixties.

But one of the more overlooked stories of this generation's mark on history is the incalculable number of one-on-one battles that individual Boomers have quietly fought in adulthood, frequently in the workplace against their Silent bosses, for their generation's values-driven and ethics-driven beliefs. An overlooked story. But every now and then, such stories bubble up to the surface:

"The country is starved for integrity"

May 21, 2002.

Colleen Rowley, a First-Wave Boomer mother of four, sole breadwinner in the family, and a woman who's only two and a half years from retirement from what everyone agrees is a distinguished career, nonetheless makes the very personal decision to put all of that – *everything* – on the line.

She testifies before the U.S. Senate Committee on Intelligence that her employer, the FBI, deliberately ignored alerts and obstructed investigations by its Minneapolis office that might have helped to uncover the terror attacks of September 11, 2001, before they occurred.

TIME magazine will later choose Rowley, and two other women – Boomer Sherron Watkins and Boomer Cynthia Cooper – as its 2002 Persons of the Year. Watkins risks everything to reveal the executive corruption at Enron. And Cooper does the same to expose the executive corruption at WorldCom.

In a *Des Moines Register* story about Rowley a month after the *TIME* tribute was published, reporter Mary Challender summed up Rowley's courage this way: "When you're called to stand, you stand, even if your legs are shaking." And Rowley herself, speaking to middle and high school students in her tiny hometown of New Hampton, Iowa, told them, "The country is starved for integrity."

Classic Boomer idealism. Doing what she did because, simply, *it's the right thing to do.*

Forever young

Boomers truly are the forever young generation; they really do think young, without trying and without being especially aware of it.

"Mommy Loudest"

The Wall Street Journal and *People* magazine have written stories about the increase in the number of Boomer mothers who are forming their own rock bands and who schedule weekend nightclub performances around their career and mommy schedules. One Boomer rocker muttered a Boomer mantra when she looked around at her suburban housewife life one day and found herself saying, *"This can't be all there is."*

Some of the names of these Boomer mother bands:

- From Detroit, *The Mydols.*
- From New York City, *Housewives on Prozac.*
- And only from our Boomer sisters out in wonderfully wacky California would we get a Boomer mother band that chooses to call itself *The Lactators.*

They have their own three-day rock and roll festival in New York. It's called Mamapalooza.

To Boomers, the battle cry from this day forward is simple: Aging is mandatory. But growing old is *optional.*

Science and medicine and their own core values are permitting Boomers to continue to rewrite the *Book of Life.*

We're in a golden era of anti-aging science because Boomers are a massive generation, with massive spending power and that forever young mindset. So they are likely to deliver a spectacular return on investment to whichever corporation or government agency or individual scientist finds a way to slow, stop, and reverse the aging process.

And at every future age marker – 65, 85, and yep 125 – Boomers are about to dramatically alter the lifestyle model, the career model, and the consumer model from what they've always been before at those same age markers.

"… a marketer's dream"

A 2005 *BusinessWeek* magazine cover shouts out the truth:

"Love Those Boomers! Their new attitudes and lifestyles are a marketer's dream."

A massive revolution in the consumer marketplace is underway right now. Some marketers get it and are cashing in. Some marketers are behind the times and blowing it.

The money is going north of age fifty at an astonishing pace. But even more important, that money is available to marketers and advertisers because of these four documented truths:

Not brand loyal
Disproportionate spending power
Free spending
Receptive to advertising

- Boomers are not brand loyal, never have been, and never will be. And in the American marketplace, that puts the Boomers "in play."
- Boomers already control a disproportionate amount of this country's wealth. In addition, they are now beginning to receive the largest transfer of wealth in human history, as their parents – the first generation of Americans to benefit from Social Security and entitlement programs from the 1930s and '40s – pass away and bequeath their estates to their children.
- Boomers are still instant-gratification free spenders.
- And they are receptive to advertising.

And this changes just about everything.

A Roper/ASW research study, conducted for AARP, finally documented this sea change in 2001.

It is a lengthy research study but here's the bottom-line finding: *"Americans 45-plus, contrary to conventional wisdom, are no more brand loyal than younger people in most categories."*

The study concludes: *"With the exception of only a few categories, the majority of 45-plus Americans are not loyal to any one brand."*

So, we've now walked through the unique formative years of the Boomers. We have a feel for the unique core values that were molded during their unique formative years.

And here are just a few examples of how some marketers have used this knowledge to craft some very savvy Boomer messaging.

Walt Disney World

Let's say you're on the marketing and advertising team at Walt Disney World in Orlando, Florida.

It's 2001, the one-hundred-year anniversary of the birth of founder Walt Disney. You want to seize the moment. You want to lure visitors to the park for a yearlong celebration of Mr. Disney.

You decide to go after this massive generation, now mostly in its forties and fifties. And you create a thirty-second

TV spot that homes in on these forever young Boomers.

How do you do it? How can you get this generation's attention with a television spot?

**Forever young
free spirited, boisterous
comfortable in the spotlight.
Competitive, like to finish first.**

Well, the research documents that Boomers' formative years molded core values of:

- forever young.
- free spirited, exuberant, boisterous – if you blink your eyes, Boomers will take over the whole doggoned event!
- they don't mind being center stage; Boomers have been in the spotlight all their lives.
- they're competitive, they like to win, they like to be #1, they like to finish "first."
- Eureka! Boomers were Disney's *first* generation.

The TV commercial opens with a wide camera shot of a school spelling bee in a hushed auditorium. With an audience of Baby Boomer parents and grandparents watching and listening in perfect stillness, we hear the PA announcer instruct the pigtailed elementary-school girl standing nervously alone on stage in front of a microphone to "spell microphone."

She slowly and carefully begins spelling microphone. "M-I-C" –

Suddenly from the audience, a gray-haired Boomer male interrupts, jumping out of his seat, turning to the other audience members, and continuing the spelling, but now of a different word: "K-E-Y!"

All Boomers in the audience instantly stand, twirl, and raucously break in to their childhood anthem: "M-O-U-S-E! Mickey Mouse! Donald Duck! Forever let us hold our banner high! High! High! High!"

To the astonishment – and bewilderment – of the young girl at the microphone and a young boy shown in the audience, the Boomers are now out of control, even the Boomer judges, dancing with each other, grinning and laughing, eleven years old once again, as they finish the song at the top of their lungs.

Instantly, the spot cuts to outdoor shots at Walt Disney World, where Boomers are dancing with Disney characters (Goofy!) with a big crowd surrounding them, as the off-camera announcer begins the sales pitch asking them to come to the park: "You were Disney's first generation. Come be a kid again...."

I show this spot in my training seminars, and audiences coast to coast love it. Boomers laugh and applaud when they watch it. Silent and Xer and Millennial audience members nod their heads in agreement. *Yep, that's the Boomers.*

Powerful generation-specific "creative" from the folks at Disney World.

Boston Pops Orchestra
Baby Boomer Bash Concert Series

Generational Event Marketing:

The Boston Pops Orchestra concluded a robust summer tour a few years back, with a generation-themed concert it took to seven cities.

It was called the Baby Boomer Bash Concert series. I called the Pops' PR director afterward, and he said attendance was incredible. Free media coverage was incredible.

The Boomers broke attendance records in order to hear the Pops play the music of the Beatles, Carole King, and Simon and Garfunkel, and to sing along with music they had heard on the Saturday morning TV cartoon shows of their childhood days.

A quick point for those of you in public relations:

The legitimate *print* media – your daily newspapers, the national news magazines, and others – have demonstrated a very enthusiastic interest in writing generations-related stories, especially newspapers.

So if you're looking for free media possibilities, examine legitimate generational angles for your project or announcement or news advisory and then write your news releases along generational lines.

When the Pops announced its Baby Boomer Bash concert series, the *Cincinnati Enquirer* wrote two full pages in its lifestyle section on this generationally strategized event. And the concert didn't even come to Cincinnati.

Morgan Stanley

With one of its print ads, Morgan Stanley connects very effectively with Boomer core values of assertiveness, willingness to take control, devotion to their parents, and that Boomer optimism.

The photo in the ad is a cozy, living room setting, showing two well-worn leather chairs and a table and lamp and a few books on a shelf, clearly at the home of the Boomers' G.I. or Silent parents. No people are shown, just the furniture. The copy reads:

"Mom, Dad, have a seat. There's something we've got to talk about. Should you sell your house and buy a smaller place? Live with us? Or travel forever and ever and ever? Don't worry. We'll figure it all out."

Boomers – aggressive, assertive, protective of their parents, and eternally optimistic – are often involved in decisions about Mom and/or Dad.

Industries such as assisted-living and retirement communities, health care, financial services, and others that target G.I.s and Silents are now marketing directly to their assertive Boomer kids, especially with direct mail.

Taylor Guitars

The guitar industry has enjoyed a recent uptick in sales because Boomers, relentlessly experiential and always wanting to learn something new, have the time and money to develop a new skill. And bunches of them apparently want to be rock and rollers!

Taylor guitars created a national-award-winning print ad.

The photo shows a balding Boomer guy, wearing a tank top T-shirt and strumming an acoustic guitar as he stands outdoors *in snow*. The copy reads:

"You're right. You're probably too late to get into the Rock and Roll Hall of Fame. But you're never too late to give the world another cover version of *Smoke on the Water*."

And this copy brings us to a critical point about messaging to Boomers:

- It does not say "you're too old"; it doesn't even say "you're too late."

- It says you're probably – *probably* – too late to get into the Rock and Roll Hall of Fame. And that speaks to that buoyant Boomer optimism: *Oh, okay, probably too late, right? Well that's all I need to hear – I've got a chance! I'm goin' for the Hall of Fame!!"*

When messaging to Boomers, *never say never,* there's always hope!

Speaking of "never," when dealing with Boomers, never, never, never refer to Boomers in these terms:

- **Senior Citizen** – A noble label for G.I.s and Silents, but a deal breaker to Boomers.
- **Retirement/Retiree** – Boomers will never fully retire.
- **Aging** – Ohmygod, noooooooooooooooooooooooooo!
- **Elderly** – Dittoooooooooooooooooooooooooooooo!
- **Golden Years** – A label for "my parents' generation."
- **Silver Years** – Ditto. In fact, no references to *any* precious metals.
- **Prime Time** – *Every day of their lives* has been prime time. Don't get *cute.*
- **Mature** – Never insult Boomers by calling them "mature."

When I presented these "never" terms at a national transportation conference in Stevenson, Washington, one audience member returned to work and e-mailed a summary of the conference to her colleagues working for the City of Seattle, "What I especially liked were Chuck Underwood's seven dirty words (at the time, I had forgotten to include an eighth word, "elderly") when marketing to Boomers." The Seven Dirty Words is the title of the legendary routine by stand-up comedian George Carlin and his Seven Words You Can Never Say on Television.

Within a couple of weeks, *Arizona Republic* reporter Susan Felt had written a story about this *new* list of dirty words, when messaging to the Boomers.

AARP

The nice folks at the American Association of Retired Persons (AARP) surely must have begun drooling out of both corners of their mouths in 1996. The leading edge of the massive Boomer Generation was now reaching AARP membership age, fifty.

Hallelujah!! Here comes the Boomer tidal wave, we're gonna be flush with members and cash!

Boomers avoided AARP like the plague.

You want ME to join an organization called the American Association of Retired Persons!? Are you kidding me?! You want to mail me your magazine called "Modern Maturity"? I'd be mortified if my neighbors saw the mailman putting that thing in my mailbox!

And so, profound change was required for this important advocacy organization. It officially changed its name to simply its acronym – AARP, which minimizes the phrase "Retired Persons" that Boomers recoil from.

AARP took the additional and significant step of launching a completely separate magazine, just for Boomers. In fact, at one point, AARP published three versions of its magazine for its various fifty-plus age cohorts.

Instead of *Modern Maturity*, AARP titled its Boomer version *My Generation*. Different editorial content, meant for Boomers. Boomer-targeted advertising, graphics, everything. But later, it unified *My Generation* – and all of its versions – under the single title *AARP The Magazine*, the organization has simply built too much brand equity in that acronym over the years to dilute it with multiple titles. By spring of 2006, readership by First-Wave Boomers had increased 12 percent, and this was during an era when the rest of the magazine industry was struggling with declining circulation and ad revenues.

In 2007, AARP is planning a new marketing campaign, new logo, enhanced Web presence, sponsorship of music concerts and television programming, and more. It must "grow young" if it wants to get Boomers.

AARP and Boomers, in principle, *should* be a powerhouse marriage waiting to happen. Both are social-change advocates. Both feel they can take on government and other major institutions, when necessary, and *win*. This is a beautiful marriage of clout, empowerment, and engagement waiting to happen *if* AARP makes effective use of generational strategy to connect with Boomers.

Cadillac

In the early '80s, Cadillac sales began to languish.

The oldest Boomers had reached luxury car age and weren't buying Cadillacs, which to them represented the snobbery, the show of wealth, the class status symbol that First-Wave Boomers had grown up to despise. Perhaps even more importantly, Cadillac also meant *old people*.

So Boomers went to Japanese luxury cars, whose sales soared. And Cadillac suffered through two decades of what *The Wall Street Journal* politely described as "lagging" sales.

Then in 2002, as *The Wall Street Journal* reported, Cadillac sales increased 16 percent in that one year, biggest gain in nearly two decades.

Cadillac did it with Boomer-targeted product design – its husky CTS model – and an advertising campaign so very different from the way Cadillac had always presented its product.

With its design of the CTS model, Cadillac nostalgically returned Boomers to the muscle car era that had been such a huge part of their formative years in the '60s and early '70s.

And instead of accentuating wealth and power and country club snobbery, its TV commercials focused upon engine power and speed and "young," as one TV spot shows the CTS screaming down a dusty old country road with background music by Led Zeppelin. This generationally savvy campaign was a huge success. And the generationally-designed CTS goes down in history as "the car that saved Cadillac".

"This is not your father's Oldsmobile"

In the late 1980s, Oldsmobile suffered from the same malaise as Cadillac (and Chrysler and Buick). Boomers perceived it as *my father's car*. So Oldsmobile mounted a full frontal attack with an advertising campaign anchored by a tag-line that left no doubt whatsoever the ad was meant for Boomers. The memorable tagline to the campaign was:

"This is not your father's Oldsmobile."

So Boomers noticed the ads, took a look at the 1988 Oldsmobile, maybe even test-drove it, and made their decision: *The hell it isn't.*

And Oldsmobile tanked.

Sometimes, you have to change more than your slogan.

GAP

One of the more explicit users of generational strategy has been the GAP.

In 2003, men's apparel sales in the United States were down 2 percent from the year before, and women's apparel sales were down 6 percent. The GAP was up 4 percent. And a *Wall Street Journal* report credited the robust sales year to the GAP's merchandise – of course – and its *multi-generational advertising campaign.*

A two-page magazine spread shows two models wearing GAP hooded sweatshirts, "hoodies." On the right is model Bridget Hall, the typical teenage-looking, very skinny, lots-of-attitude model we've seen forever in women's apparel ads. On the left is *then fifty-seven-year-old* model Lauren Hutton.

Women's apparel has historically been one of the more age-discriminatory categories in all of advertising.

But GAP launched a massive campaign using a variety of multigenerational on-camera talent in its print and television campaign. And it worked. Its slogan for this campaign?

"The GAP. For every generation."

I showed the Bridget Hall/Lauren Hutton ad to one of my own formal focus groups of ten Gen X women, in their twenties and thirties, and asked them which of the two images would be more persuasive in getting them to buy the "hoodie."

Although much closer in age to Bridget Hall, they nonetheless voted in favor of fifty-seven-year-old Lauren Hutton. What surprised me was the tally:

10-0.

I asked them, "Why?"

One replied, "She (Hutton) is beautiful and sexy, and she looks so comfortable in her own skin." Another added, "I love that she's smiling and actually flashing that gap in her front teeth. You go, girl!"

I pushed it. "Yeah, but she is *so much older than you.* You're much closer in age to the younger model."

They all shook their heads, one of them saying about the younger image, "She's trying too hard. I don't identify with her."

I pushed it some more. "Yeah, but this one (I pointed to

the older Hutton) is almost *sixty years old!*"

At that moment, they just shrugged. But a few moments later, one of the women, twenty-eight years old, said, "Do you know what sixty years old means to women my age? Tina Turner!"

Age bias in advertising is dying a swift death.

Capital One: Generational Credit Cards

The corporations that comprise the financial services industry began the new millennium locked in brutal competition to land Boomer accounts and get their hands on all that Boomer money.

Capital One created a direct-mail piece, offering what it calls its Generations MasterCard. Purchasers of the credit card may receive their card with any one of nine Boomer-nostalgic graphic images imprinted on the front: a big-finned Cadillac from the late '50s; the yellow have-a-nice-day "smiley face" that was seen everywhere in the '60s and '70s; the international peace symbol; a ticket stub from Woodstock; the silver spinning disco ball from the '70s; and others.

This is straightforward generational marketing. If you're a Boomer, it would be darned near impossible to *not* look at each of those nine images and instantly wax nostalgic.

Fidelity Investments

In another advertising campaign targeting Boomers, Fidelity Investments' print ads and TV spots show a montage of nostalgic images of Boomers throughout their youth, accompanied by copy that matches the images. One such ad shows a Boomer woman's birth photo and photos from her childhood, teen and college years, young adult, and current-day fifty-something photo. The copy reads:

"This is Carol. She's been called a hippie, preppy, yuppie, protester, Democrat, Republican, mom, CFO, CEO, cancer patient, cancer survivor, fund-raiser, spokesperson, caregiver, journalist, and soon-to-be world traveler. Reaching retirement is no small achievement. We'll help you make the most of it."

Ameriprise

And Ameriprise goes unabashedly for Boomers in its campaign, constantly inserting the word "generation" in its copy and voiceover.

"A generation as unique as this needs a new generation of financial planning." Or...

"Think the generation who lived through all this (as we see footage of fashion, protest, celebrities, and other nostalgia from the '60s and '70s) is going to go out... (camera shot of an empty rocking chair on a front porch)... like *this*? NO WAY!" The spot goes on to acknowledge that Boomers are "reinventing what retirement means" as it shows shots of energetic Boomers conducting business, traveling, and making a difference.

And Ameriprise uses a hurry-to-the-dance-floor song from the '60s in this campaign: Spencer Davis Group's "Gimme Some Lovin'."

Important point # 1 about what we've just read: pop music is the most generation-specific medium of all. If you want to really target a generation and can afford to purchase the rights to use a hit song from the youth of your targeted generation, the music can deliver instant recognition to the viewer or radio listener: *this message is meant for me.* If not the music, then perhaps a famous line from the song's lyrics?

Important point # 2: Generationally-strategized messages can do the one thing every marketer, advertiser, and ad agency desperately seeks these days – they can *cut through the clutter.* Virtually all of the generational marketing strategies mentioned in this book are magnificent examples of messaging that announces clearly and immediately to the targeted generation, *this message is for YOU.*

Generational "creative" cuts through the clutter.

Boomers: Their Future

Boomers, you're up.

There's been so much news coverage of you in the past decade, as your leading edge first turned fifty and then sixty, that many Americans assume we've *been* a Boomer

Nation for some time now.

We haven't.

In 2006 and 2007, the hand-off from the older Silent leaders to your generation is only now nearing completion. You're assuming majorities – or at least generational pluralities – atop our nation's major institutions: business, government, religion, media, education, and others.

It's your turn to install your generation's unique values in the leadership positions.

The unique times and teachings of your formative years, *beyond your generation's control*, molded in your generation virtually every key value and quality needed for truly *great* leadership. The heavens were perfectly aligned for it, like they were for the G. I. Generation, and unlike they were for Silents and Xers. Those times and teachings cemented in you Boomers a special boldness of vision, selflessness, compassion for the less fortunate, team play, idealism, ethics, a willingness to lead and to attempt the difficult and even the impossible because it's the right thing to do, a willingness to make the tough decisions and be held accountable for your actions, a passion to dream the biggest dream, a remarkable sense of empowerment and engagement, and the certainty in your belief that you can make a big difference

And nothing less than the future of America rests on the answer to one big question. It is a question bigger than the ones about our nation's war against terror, our epidemic of executive corruption, and our economic uncertainty. It goes like this:

You once had your idealistic ethics and values, your passion, your empowerment and engagement. And this means *both* of you First Wave and Second Wave Boomers.

Do you still?

You believed in bettering life for the masses, not just the privileged few, and you believed in People Power because for one brief shining moment you proved *it works.*

Do you still?

You were fearless, willing to try a better way, willing to risk failure.

Are you still?

Or, in order to advance your careers while working for older bosses the past thirty years, have you relinquished your idealism in favor of pragmatism, simply to get along in a workplace culture dictated by a different generation?

Or even more simply, have you sold out, and are you now in it for "me"?

And about your belief back then that this is the one nation on Earth with the best chance to *get everything right...*

Were you wrong? Or, is it still?

As you take your turn at the top, most surveys document that Americans feel your generation is inheriting a leadership culture that is the ethical and moral equivalent of a toxic waste dump. They think their nation is one big mess. Americans are disheartened and feel stripped of their empowerment.

Remember what Boomer and 2002 *TIME* magazine co-person of the year Colleen Rowley said? "The country is starved for integrity."

By about the year 2017, after you've had a good solid decade holding down most of the executive suites of America's major institutions, you will have installed Boomer values in America's leadership positions. And only then will America learn for certain the answer to the one question upon which the future of this nation rests.

How much of you is left, Boomers?

Chapter 6

Marketing To Boomers
Tips, tactics, and guidelines

REMEMBER:

However you've previously marketed to prior generations of forty- and fifty- and sixty-somethings…

Change it.

Now.

The American youth culture that began with the Baby Boomers is now ending with the Baby Boomers.

Oh sure, marketers will still pursue youth, but no longer to the exclusion of fifty-plus. Boomers are wealthy, free spending, open to new products and services, not brand loyal, and receptive to advertising. And this opens up *everything*.

The population of this generation is huge. Its purchasing power is staggering. And remember, you're in business to do three things:

1. Follow the money.
2. Follow the money.
3. Follow the money.

As if that were not enough, Boomers are now beginning to receive the largest transfer of wealth in human history – the inheritances from their G.I. and Silent Generation parents. Estimates on the total amount vary widely, but it's *at least* in the hundreds of billions.

Boomers are demanding customers.

Always keep in mind that Boomers are not blindly brand loyal. Never have been. Never will be. If they've purchased or leased five Toyotas in a row, it's not because of blind brand loyalty, it's because Toyota has earned them five separate times. Note to Toyota: don't get cocky. If Chevrolet or Honda comes along with a car that better suits their needs, Boomers will dump you in a New York minute.

Regarding brand loyalty, think about this:

The parents of First-Wave Boomers are the G.I.s and Rosie the Riveters from World War II. As Boomer kids were coming of age, they frequently heard their parents pledge to never purchase a German or Japanese car and to always be loyal to American-made autos; understandable feelings in the aftermath of the war. (Millennials, would you buy a car today that Al Qaeda manufactured?). So, what was the first major purchase by the Baby Boom Generation?

The German-made Volkswagen Beetle.

And with that consumer decision, this generation was announcing that all bets are off. The Beetle best suited their unique generational values: it was cheaper and more reliable and fuel-efficient than American-made cars, and it was loaded with anti-snobbery attitude.

Here's the proof about brand loyalty, from that 2001 Roper/ASW research mentioned earlier:

- "Americans forty-five-plus, contrary to conventional wisdom, are no more brand loyal than younger people in most categories. And 55 percent of people forty-five-plus (compared to 58 percent of people under forty-five) agree with the statement, 'In today's marketplace, it doesn't pay to be loyal to one brand.'"

According to this study, consumers forty-five-plus are:

- *less* brand loyal than under-forty-five (!) when it comes to: home computers; cell phones; athletic footwear; stereo equipment; and, motor vehicles besides cars (e.g., SUVs).
- *equally* loyal to: skin care/cosmetics/fragrances; DVD/ video players; athletic leisurewear; casual sportswear; jewelry; and, clothing accessories.
- *more* loyal to: bath soap; cars (not SUVs) and auto parts; home appliances; TVs; cereal; vitamins; and, shoes.

The study concludes: **"With the exception of only a few categories, the majority of forty-five-plus Americans are not loyal to any one brand."**

At any age, Boomers will be receptive to advertising and marketing messages, and to new products and services. This destroys the obsolete but long-held notion that people fifty-plus cannot be influenced by advertising because they're "set in their ways."

Although receptive to advertising, Boomers are streetwise and can smell hype a mile away. So communicate your product's benefits in an honest, fact-based manner. Cut the crap.

Marketers: be careful. Because the hard-working and career-driven Boomers are now in mid- to late-career, don't fall into the trap of pitching your products and services to them with this kind of messaging: "You've worked hard, you've *earned* it, you *deserve* it, *reward* yourself." This works with the Silents, but with Boomers I advise you, "Don't do it." In a recent Boomer focus group I conducted for my own company, I was surprised at the universal response when I asked, "Are you the *most pressured* generation?"

No!, they passionately answered. "Pressure?" asked one. "Try the Great Depression, try World War Two. Whatever pressure we Boomers are feeling is *nothing* compared to what our parents and grandparents experienced." The others in the focus group agreed. *Boomers will probably never feel entitled to reward themselves.* They'll never feel like they've done *enough.* They will always measure their own right to reward themselves against that of their parents' and grandparents' generations, and they will always feel they've had it comparatively easy. If you want to sell "entitlement" and "earned the right" and "go ahead, reward yourself," sell it to the Silents. With the Boomers, this kind of messaging probably will miss.

Boomers *value values*. They're ethics driven. Your product and your company must be "right." Socially responsible. And even cause-active.

Boomers are time stressed. Many face extended elder-care with their parents and/or extended childcare with their twenty-something kids who are staying at home in bigger numbers than ever before. They're still working feverishly at their careers. As consumers, they seek *fast* and *convenient* and *no-hassle* and *reliable,* and they're willing to pay extra for it, if they must.

Credit card companies, most of your direct-mail pieces targeting Boomers stink. Too lengthy. You bury the important details. Too much hype. If you want to get Boomers (and Xers, who are also time-starved) to read the *second* sentence of your direct-mail piece, you must earn them with your first sentence. And most of you don't seem to get that. You're wasting Boomers' time, and that's a deal breaker.

Boomers have a distinct "First Wave" and "Second Wave" to their generation. The First-Wave Boomers are the social activists of the '60s. Second-wave Boomers missed out on much of the activism and came of age during the time-to-party era of the late '70s and early '80s. But they share enough common values that they are a single generation:

Strong sense of right and wrong. Confident and assertive. Demanding. Optimistic by nature. Workaholics. Great love for, and respect of, their parents. Many of them struggled with their own marriage and parenting. One newspaper headline reporting on Boomers' sense of inadequacy as parents reads: "My Mom Was a Better Mom." Many Boomers have a sense of guilt and regret that their time-poor lives have prevented them from being the kind of parents their own mothers and fathers were, and are, to them.

Boomers want to make the smartest possible purchase. They do their homework before making the bigger purchases.

Boomers are in the midst of several sizable life passages, all of which create marketplace opportunities:

- They're ascending to their peak career and earning years.
- They'll soon be, or now are, empty nesters.
- They're becoming grandparents.
- Many of them are single, often by choice.
- They're engaged in eldercare with their parents, who are living longer than ever.
- A significant number are facing extended childcare, as their adult children stay at home longer.
- Boomers have been ambushed in their careers by downsizing and executive corruption, so many are in big trouble with their retirement finances. This is now a major focus for them.
- Boomer women, an especially lucrative market, are rewriting the book about living, working, and spending as they pass through their forties and fifties and now move into their sixties.

Boomers are the forever young Generation because the America of their formative years imbued them with hope and love and optimism. And this opens up countless opportunities for marketers and advertisers.

Boomers are the workaholic generation. They have defined themselves by their careers.

TIPS, TACTICS, GUIDELINES – MARKETING TO BOOMERS

Don't use the following words when communicating to Boomers. Not now, not when they're 120 years old. Ignore this warning, and fall on your face. Never refer to the Boomer Generation and their future in these terms:

- Senior Citizen.
- Aging.
- Elderly.
- Mature.
- Retiree/Retiring.
- Golden Years.
- Silver Years.
- Prime Time.

Don't use "Life Begins at fifty." Or sixty. Tired, irrelevant, and so not-Boomer.

Don't make *any* age sound like a marker. Present life as one continual, ageless adventure.

Boomers are passionate parents and grandparents, especially because so many of them feel they botched their early attempts at marriage and parenting, and many are parenting very differently the second time around. So connect them with their families; it's a hot button. Multigenerational advertising will work with Boomers. But beware:

Arizona Republic reporter Susan Felt interviewed me for a story addressing this question: do forever young Boomers mind being called *grandmother* and *grandfather*? Well, this might give you a hint. As mentioned in Ms. Felt's story, when Boomer actress Goldie Hawn first became a grandmother she revised the label from *gramma* to *glamma*. And I'm quoted in the story as saying Boomers don't mind being called "Grandma" and "Grandpa" by their grandchildren and as long as they're not marketed to in a way that conjures up the stereotypical rocking chair image of grandparenthood. "If there can be an alternative name that doesn't attach *aging* to that life stage of grandparenthood, Boomers are certainly the generation that will embrace that name change," I said.

Boomers love *meaningful* detail. They hate *meaningless* detail.

Arrange your printed collaterals for speedy and easy consumption, like *USA Today*. Boomers are time-crunched. No time for cute and lengthy storytelling – *just the facts*.

However, *The Wall Street Journal* has just done some major reformatting and is now heading in the opposite direction, writing *longer* stories with *more* depth and comprehensiveness to those topics that require it. I hope it works and can't wait to see if it does.

Boomers and the News

Boomers are empowered and engaged, so they devour the daily newspaper and its coverage of current events, National Public Radio, the weekly news magazines, and the nightly *network* news. They understand and recognize factual and principled journalism.

But from my own qualitative research studies and from local TV ratings, they think *local* TV news is, as one Boomer focus-group participant described it, "a joke." *Our lead story at six is traffic accident # 1. Our second story is traffic accident # 2. Our third story is crime #1.* And Boomer news hounds cry out, *Where's the relevance? The importance to my life? Where's the good watchdog reporting?* To Boomers, local TV news is phony, shallow, slow paced, irrelevant to their lives, anchored by "bubble-headed bleach blondes" instead of journalists, and unworthy of their time.

This attitude towards local TV news, by the way, is multigenerational. Xers don't watch local TV news in percentages anywhere close to prior generations at their age. And from a widely-circulated report from a television-industry research firm, only one-third of adult-age Millennials claim to have a favorite TV station for news and *the more news they watch the lower their evaluation of that news station*! I've consulted more than thirty television stations, thus far. And I tell them all the same thing: local television news, in the late 2000s, is marching full-throttle into irrelevance and unimportance, a crisis that is going to get worse, not better, without major transformation of its story selection, pace, presentation, and training in the generational influences on viewing decisions. And to be candid, in 2007 I see little movement by television news in the direction of that transformation. With only a precious few exceptions, I see too many attempts at cheap shortcuts and promotional trickery to try to sell viewers on the importance of local TV news.

And how's this for a story about The Absolute Opposite: daily newspapers, more than ever, are the singular source for The Best Obtainable Version Of The Truth, the only trustworthy source of comprehensive explanations of the daily events in our hometowns, states, nation, and world. Unlike local TV news, whose *product* is considered so feeble, the newspapers' actual *product* is more impressive and essential than ever, as Americans want and need to stay current on so many issues and events impacting their lives. But where television is slick at *promoting* its product, newspapers stink at promotion and are losing readership, especially with MTV-Generation Xers, despite the importance and general excellence of its product! I consult the newspaper industry, too. And I tell them, "Your product is more needed than ever. But you must launch a generationally-strategized educational campaign, not merely a marketing or promotional campaign, to teach or re-teach Americans of the journalistic integrity and necessity of your product." The newspaper industry is moving far too slowly in effecting this needed change. Its problem is generational, so its solution is generational.

Are you planning to give Boomers your business card? If so, what type size and color contrast are on your card? Is it reader friendly or have you decided to express your creative side with a user-unfriendly, impossible-to-read, but good-looking card? Screw *good-looking*. Use big-enough type and sharp-enough color contrast. Don't test the type size on a twenty-five-year-old employee. Show the design to Boomers, get their thoughts. Explain to your artist, who understandably might want to design your card for looks rather than user friendliness, that – first and foremost – you seek *user friendly*.

Point-of-sale signage and takeaways, done right, are a key convenience to a generation that considers itself time poor. Boomers want to quickly get in and out of the store, the gym, the doctor's office, and the auto dealer, *but* still having made smart purchases. *Make it easy for them to be smart.*

Don't get so carried away with your Web site's creative design that you slow the download of your home page. Visually interesting, yes. But never, never, never slow it down "too much," not with Boomers (and Xers and Millennials). Your home page should download swiftly. Save the heavy video and graphics for interior pages. Ad agencies, you are the absolute worst at this:

Loading... Loading... Loading... Skip This Intro?

Hell, yes, skip the intro!!!

Boomer women tend to look more excitedly and optimistically at their future than Boomer men do. Likely reason why: women foresee a long list of adventures awaiting them when they finally empty-nest and leave their first careers. Boomer men, who have defined themselves so thoroughly by the careers, see approaching retirement as an unclear and perhaps unsettling passage. The message? Capture that sense of celebration in Boomer women's next passage. Help the Boomer men to feel still valuable, and excited, about their futures too.

Boomer Hot Buttons: forever young; help them with their finances; help them to connect with their children and grandchildren; help them to continue their passion to make a positive difference on Planet Earth.

Travel deserves a special mention: the travel industry is right-on to pursue the Boomers, who want experiential and learning vacations, not simply flopping on the beach for a week. But travel, according to recent research, is not yet a high priority for Boomers because of time, career, family, and financial constraints on their lives. But when they do travel, they travel quite differently from Silents and G.I.s. One such difference is captured in a recent *Wall Street Journal* headline, "Boomers to cruise industry: less cruising!" Boomers don't want to lie on a deck chair for nine days of circling the Caribbean islands. They want to get *off* the ship and immerse themselves in the authenticity of the islands' native cultures. And they want to be physically active while on the ship.

Double-check your own staffers: are they all younger than Boomers? If so, they might not accurately relate to Boomer consumer attitudes and might be guilty of stereotyping and guessing. It's a new world. Hire a Boomer. Or three. Remember that earlier quote from marketing firm Weber Shandwick? "Marketers must reorient forty years of thinking."

Boomers remain the Golden Demographic because of their enormous body count, their awesome purchasing power, and their instant-gratification core value.

Boomers don't possess "generation envy." They like being Boomers, and they like their current life stage. They're not desperate to be nineteen again. Here are a couple of right-on taglines in Boomer-female advertising:

- Clairol: "A Beauty All Your Own."
- Victoria's Secret: "At last, I'm comfortable."

- And this actual brand name, "Not Your Daughter's Jeans": "Made for real women, with real curves."

A newspaper reporter called me to get the generational angle to the recent surge in sales of Harley-Davidson motorcycles, and he asked this question with cynicism dripping from every word: "Isn't this nothing more than a desperate attempt by an aging generation to try to fool itself into thinking it's younger than it is?" I replied, "You don't get it. Boomers – men and women – are not buying Harleys to try to recapture their youth. They're buying Harleys because they can't wait for this Saturday's ride into the country and next summer's vacation across America."

Boomers are as *future oriented* as any generation can be. Life is not about yesterday. Yesterday was magnificent, yes. But everything with Boomers is about seizing the *next* moment. Life is one long banquet table to Boomers, and they want to sample every dish.

If you try to turn the Boomers into an oldies' act, as some television producers and marketers are now doing, *you will lose*. With this generation, it will always be about *tomorrow*.

Real Estate:

- Boomers want choices. Builders know they can't tell Boomers what they want. Boomers will tell them. Give them lots of options, builders. Listen, don't talk.
- They might live in their wrongly-named "retirement homes" for thirty or more years!
- Many are not doing the traditional downsizing as they become empty nesters. Instead? *More* space for offices,

home theater, bigger bedrooms and bathrooms and
hallways and in-law suites that one day might need to
be retrofitted with grab bars and for wheelchair access. No steps. Extra bedrooms for the grandkids and
great grandkids. And so on.
- And Boomers in cold-weather climates are apparently
not going to flee to the Sun Belt like prior generations. Many will stay put *to be near their families*. However,
those who have the money might do the *second-home*
thing in a warm climate.

As Grandparents:

- Like Silents, Boomers increasingly participate in the
primary care of grandchildren and so also participate
in the purchasing decisions associated with it.
- As grandparents, Boomers place a premium on the
grandkids' safety, education, and shared experiences, and this will show up in their purchases for their
grandkids.

Finances:

- In 2006, The Center for Retirement Research at
Boston College asked 400 employers to gauge the retirement readiness of workers fifty and older. The bottom line: at least one quarter of First-Wave Boomers
will lack the resources to retire at the traditional age
and will need to work at least two years beyond it.
- This instant-gratification generation knows it needs
help from financial planners. Those who get the
Boomers where they want to go without great sacrifice
(perhaps not possible, in some cases) will win.

Varilux case study:

Presbyopia is an eyesight affliction. Varilux offers eye-glasses to relieve the condition. It ran a recent TV campaign that presented a fictional 1960s-style protest by the *Presbyopic Six* (harkens back to the Chicago Seven of 1960s political protest fame), who protest and carry signs about their "right to see" and are arrested. This campaign humorously captures the social activism of the Boomers by showing sit-ins and protest songs.

Boomers admire their parents. They know the devotion and selflessness Mom and Dad gave to raising them. Use this powerful, emotional tie. Apparel retailer Land's End put Rosie the Riveter on a recent cover. In Boomers, that image stirs powerful memories of their G.I. Generation moms working in the factories and offices during World War II to help the war effort. Similar images capturing their parents' generation can resonate with grateful Boomer kids.

Internet. Boomers initially used the Internet for hard information: their purchases, job searches, research at work. But they're beginning to use it more for entertainment, especially since a good portion of commercial television and radio – and advertisers – seem to be abandoning Boomers for younger generations of listeners and viewers. So Boomers are doing a little gaming on the Web. And Monster.com founder Jeff Taylor recently launched eons.com, described in *BusinessWeek* magazine as "MySpace for Baby Boomers." The online dating firms are now pursuing all those single Boomers. And so on. The Internet is now pursuing Boomers.

Chapter 7

Boomers In The Workplace
Tips, tactics, and guidelines

Boomers at work

- The career-driven generation.*
- Coworker relationships are important.**
- Work = vitality = engagement.
- Ethics and values are important.***
- Assertive, aggressive.****
- There's a Boomer-Xer "aggressiveness gap."*****

* According to a 2005 Merrill Lynch survey of more than three thousand Boomers, and reported in a 2006 story in *BusinessWeek* magazine, *83 percent plan to work beyond normal retirement* and 56 percent of that 83 percent hope to do so in a *new profession!*

** Boomers, like Silents, are a socially skilled "people" generation. When you couple that with their career drive, you can understand why Boomers frequently socialize with, and become personal friends with, their coworkers. Gen Xers are different and often compartmentalize their coworkers and their personal friends. A Gen X woman, in a recent seminar audience, shared this story with me, with disgust in her voice: "I had just begun work with an insurance company, and a Boomer coworker came up to me on my *first day* with a cup of coffee, and do you know what she wanted to do?!! She wanted to *have a chat*!!" Xers like to come to work, sit at their cubicle and do the job, and go home. Boomers like to get acquainted, and they'll work a few minutes past quitting time to make up the time. No right or wrong here. Just different generational core values. Not a problem if everyone is trained in generational workforce diversity.

*** A recent public television show gives a perfect example of the difference between Silent and Boomer corporate executives. In front of an auditorium audience, two powerful executives sat in overstuffed chairs, discussing modern-day business: Procter & Gamble's Boomer CEO A.G. Lafley and Fifth Third Bank's Silent CEO George Schaefer. An audience member asked, "What do the two of you look for when hiring Gen Xers?" Schaefer gave the classic *Silent* executive answer: "I'm looking for capitalists." Lafley gave the classic *Boomer* executive answer: "Integrity."

**** Boomers, a massive generation, *had* to grow up competitive with each other – aggressive. So they're comfortable with others who are the same way. Boomers *expect* others to push back hard when they disagree with them. The much smaller Gen X will never face the same kind of competition and tends to be a little less aggressive in the workplace. Many of my human resource clients repeat this same frustration: "If a Boomer employee is dissatisfied for some reason, she'll come right to the boss and fight for what she wants. But when Xers become dissatisfied, we don't hear about it until, one day out of nowhere, they give us their two-week notice!"

***** Note to Boomers: Be careful that your natural assertiveness doesn't overwhelm, dominate, and suffocate those Xers who won't fight back as vigorously as you fully expect – and *want* – them to. Don't fall into the easy trap of dominating the dialogue around the conference table. Note to Xers: It's okay to make your point assertively. To Boomers, that's normal. Fight fair, but fight hard for what you believe. Again, there's no right or wrong with either style. It's just important to understand why the generations bring different values and attitudes to the job each day.

- Leaders.*
- Care about company, all employees.
- Fair play for all.
- Pay dues.
- Play by the rules, but challenge the rules.

* If you compile a list of attributes that are essential to great leadership, you'll probably place a check mark beside every one of them when evaluating the Boomer Generation. Hard workers. Willing to go the extra mile. Team players. Excellent interpersonal skills. Loyal to, and concerned about the entire organization and all employees, not just themselves. Bold, visionary, assertive. Willing to take risks. Willing to risk failure. Willing to be accountable for their actions. Ethical. Etc., etc. It's simple: beyond their own control, the formative years of this generation – the times and teachings they absorbed

back then – just happened to mold core values perfectly suited for leadership, just as the formative years of the G.I. Generation had done. Silents have not given us a bumper crop of great leaders, and it's likely Xers won't either, *and that's okay.* Silents and Xers seem to be especially skilled at *executing* and *implementing* the visions of their just-older generations. After hearing this in my recent presentation in Washington, D.C. to representatives of the Veterans Administration Medical Centers in our country, a Gen X surgeon came up and said what other Xer audience members around the country have repeated to me: "I don't think our generation *wants* to lead," she said. "I think our values and attitudes line up perfectly for execution and implementation. Leadership doesn't hold a lot of prestige for us, because leaders were pretty rotten when we were growing up."

- Outgoing, dynamic personalities.*
- Comfortable with technology.
- Usually comfortable with change.
- Team builders.
- Wisdom from varied experiences.
- Loaded with "practical intelligence."**
- At this stage in their lives, might seek growth, not just income.
- More mobile and flexible than younger generations with their family commitments?

* Boomers are usually good "front" people for an organization. Articulate, sturdy, streetwise, comfortable in the spotlight's glare. They can take the heat. Sometimes, though, their generation's assertiveness might not be as politically correct as that of Silents.

** The white Silent male has enjoyed that remarkably smooth career passage. But many Boomers have endured more rough-and-tumble careers. The good news from this: Boomers have seen so much, experienced so much, been forced to create and survive and think outside the square. And this kind of practical intelligence is now cherished by American business.

Recruiting Boomers

- Are your management, Human Resources, and leadership personnel fully trained in Generational Workforce Diversity and Strategy across all generations? This should be imperative training for all such personnel.*
- Create a workplace culture that welcomes and values Boomers – and Silents too.
- Do your younger recruiters and managers understand the talents and preferences of these mature workers?

* Each year, for the past several years, the six Veterans Administration Medical Centers of Ohio have sent a total of thirty employees – 5 from each facility – who have been identified as future leaders to a single location for a week of leadership training. Each year, that training includes my half-day seminar in Generational Workforce Diversity and Human Resource Strategy. Management and leaders must be trained in this.

- Retirement security is a priority. Recruit Boomers with this in mind.*
- Explain the organization's big picture.

- Explain short-term and long-term goals.
- Prove that the organization is ethical.
- Discuss fulfillment, personal growth.
- Buzzword Bias?**

* Many members of this instant-gratification generation have not saved adequately for retirement. Can you help them to make up for lost time: more pay for longer hours? Creative benefit plans? More reward for more risk?

** (I've copied and pasted this paragraph from the Silent section of this book). From a health care client of mine comes this alert. He told me his organization had discovered that, in its recruiting of new talent, it had fallen victim to Buzzword Bias. That is, employees used a bunch of new buzzwords that weren't especially important, but recruiters had been evaluating candidates partially on the candidates' knowledge of this unimportant jargon. Younger generations tended to know the buzzwords, older generations didn't. And they finally realized they had lost some talented candidates for the stupidest of reasons. So, put your entire recruitment process under the microscope. Are you guilty of needless Buzzword Bias in your recruitment ads, screening, interviewing, and evaluation?

And there's another type of Buzzword Bias. Check your own job recruitment ads. Do they seek "eager to learn" and "lots of energy" applicants, or do they also welcome "experience" and "maturity"?? Are your ads instantly alienating a generation of ideal candidates?

Managing and retaining Boomers

- Train Boomers – especially management – in Generational Workforce Diversity.
- Consider new work arrangements: part-time, flextime, job sharing, leave sharing, telecommuting or "portable jobs," phased retirement, part-time projects, full benefits for part-timers, etc.
- Consider new and customized benefit, compensation, and perquisite packages: match them to Boomers' current and pending life stages. College-selection counseling for their kids and them?
- Give them choice and flexibility.
- Include them in all new training.
- Don't lower performance standards for them: "coasting toward retirement" is not an option.
- Promote or move them laterally.*
- Review your physical spaces and work schedules for possible aging unfriendliness.**
- Can you offer a comprehensive "wellness" program: education and services that will serve this generation's passion for remaining physically, mentally, and emotionally fit?

* At this stage, Boomers might enjoy re-stimulation with a lateral move to a new assignment. Don't assume you must advance them upward towards management.

** Don't patronize Boomers as they age. With respectful discretion, accommodate the likely need for larger type size, good lighting, comfortable seating, regular breaks during long meetings, and so on.

To Avoid the Boomer Brain Drain

- Aggressive recruitment and retention.*
- Can you help to reduce their stress and burnout?
- Phased retirement, for those who want to retire over several years.**
- Create a program to *systematically* transfer Boomers' (and Silents') knowledge to the next generations; ask Boomers/Silents to develop this program.

* It's not enough to "try" to recruit and retain Boomers. This must be a skilled, well-thought-out program. You are now officially in fierce competition for this generation.

** But don't "ease" them toward retirement. They don't want it. Mediocre performance is not an option for them, so it shouldn't be for your organization. It's phased *retirement*, not phased *performance*.

Chapter 8

GenX

All about survival

FORMATIVE YEARS, CORE VALUES,
ADULTHOOD, FUTURE

**Born: 1965 to 1981
58,541,842 born
Formative Years: '70s/'80s/'90s**

Generation X. It is not a derogatory label. It was popularized, not by older generations who disliked Xer attitudes,
but instead by an Xer himself named Douglas Coupland,
who wrote the novel *Generation X* in 1991. Also, punk rocker Billy Idol, for a time, had a band named Generation X.
And there were other references to it around the same
time that Coupland's book was published.

The premise is this:

This generation is so individualistic in its thinking and so
diverse in its ethnicities and lifestyles that it tends to resist

any single label, and it resents attempts by marketers and advertisers to pigeonhole it.

Born between 1965 and 1981. After a recent seminar, a Gen X woman, approaching her forties, walked up to me with a sad look on her face. She explained that she had just purchased satellite radio for her car, only to learn the brutal reality that the "music of her youth" is now considered *classic* alternative rock.

The all-important formative years for Gen X will be essentially the '70s, '80s, '90s, and early 2000s.

Fewer than fifty-nine million Xers born, according to the U. S. Census Bureau. Like the Silents, this is a pretty small generation. The Boomers, by contrast, are eighty million, as are the younger Millennials.

But the Xer birth years are occurring:

(1) just as the birth control pill is gaining widespread use;

(2) just as abortion is legalized in 1973, the ninth of this generation's seventeen birth years;

(3) and, just as the feminist movement is opening career doors for women, a number of whom are choosing to delay or completely forgo child-bearing.

The "Slacker" Thing

No American generation will grow up more isolated from

– and more misunderstood by – older generations than Gen X.

A *TIME* magazine cover story from 1997 says it all, as far as many Xers are concerned. The cover reads:

"You called us slackers. You dismissed us as Generation X. Well, move over. We're not what you thought."

As a generation, Xer children experience the most materialistically comfortable childhood to that point in American history. Thanks to the women's movement, their parents are the first generation of parents to enjoy widespread dual-*career* household incomes, not just dual-*job* incomes.

But Xers also experience the most psychologically difficult childhood in American history, as one adult institution after another fails to deliver on its promise to them.

You need to be forewarned. The formative years' stories of the Silents and Boomers are largely upbeat and optimistic stories. But the story of Gen X is a darker story. Gen Xers are born and raised when oftentimes it isn't easy being a kid in America.

But thanks to their spunk and grit and moxie, this story will have a happier ending.

Here we go....

"All about survival"

Neil Howe, who's coauthored several books about the history of America's generations, made this point as a featured guest on that one-hour television special about the generations that I produced and hosted in 2001: Generation X, he said, "has been all about survival."

It's because their formative years are influenced by four unprecedented experiments by their parents' generations; and most parents of Xers are either younger Silents or older Boomers:

Experiment # 1 - widespread divorce: According to U.S. Census Bureau statistics, in 1971, as the first Xers turn six, the divorce rate in our country is 165 percent higher than it had been only ten years earlier. And the divorce rate will climb throughout the formative years of Gen X. According to a study released in *American Demographics* magazine in the mid-'90s, 40 percent of Xers will come of age in divorced or single-parent households.

Anecdote: I presented generational training workshops to the management, marketing, and human resource teams of Zondervan, the world's largest publisher of Bibles and Christian books and gifts. One of its employees, a Gen X woman named Jen Abbas, had just coauthored the book *Generation EX: Adult Children of Divorce and Healing Our Pain.* Jen kindly mailed a copy to me, with her own hand-written note that hints at this generation's strong desire to be understood by older generations: "Chuck, thanks for all you're doing to tell our story."

Here's a passage from Jen's book, as she writes intimately

to those fellow Xers whose formative years were influenced by their parents' divorces:

"Can you identify?
- You're afraid of falling in love but really want to.
- You've turned into a perfectionist.
- You're afraid that even though someone says, 'I love you,' ultimately that person might leave you.
- For you, trust comes in hard-earned degrees.
- You're not sure where home is, or you aren't so sure you want to accept the home that society has defined for you.
- You wonder if you will ever have your entire family in the same room without fighting or awkward silence.
- You have holes in your history.
- You aren't sure what a healthy marriage looks like.

"Betrayal. Rejection. Fear. Anger. Abandonment."

Well, the one piece of good news here is that 60 percent of Xers will come of age with their nuclear families *intact*. And this is a good time to explain how *generation-wide* core values are created.

Do the math. In virtually every Gen X classroom, from kindergarten to high school senior, eight of every twenty students are coming to school each day from divorced or single-parent households. And the other twelve, who come from traditional households, sit shoulder to shoulder with those eight, class after class, cafeteria lunch after cafeteria lunch, social event after social event, throughout all of their formative years, and so they *all* become sensitized to the consequences of unhappy marriages and divorce. And so they *all* tend to mold similar core values and beliefs about marriage, divorce, family, parenting, and so on.

The *classroom* is the great incubator – the great compressor – of coast-to-coast, generation-wide core values.

Experiment # 2 - widespread career moms: Young adult women are getting their first legitimate career chance in U.S. history. And dual-career parents create our first generation of latchkey kids, Xers who must come home after school to an empty house because Mom and Dad are still at work.

The parents of Xer kids *want* to get everything right: parenting, marriage, careers. But they are the first parents in post-women's movement America.

Translation? They have no "manual" to guide them through these epic changes in career and family. So they become the generation of parents that must *write* the manual, through trial-and-error experimentation. And this trial and error is taking place as a generation of children is trying to come of age. The parents get some things right, and as they will later acknowledge they get some things wrong.

They're making more household income than prior generations, but it's costing them time with their children. As more than one parent of Gen X children has said – and felt – in the years since, "We gave them everything but ourselves."

Experiment # 3 - this new parenting era of *permissiveness*: the desire by parents to be their own children's buddies and friends rather than strict disciplinarians, where many of the rules are now negotiable and there is much less of a relentless and "preachy" parental message of right-and-wrong than what prior generations had absorbed.

When the parents of Xers (younger Silents and older Boomers) were children themselves, American neighborhoods were safe and nurturing, radio and TV shows weren't yet vulgar and exploitive but instead reinforced the parents' own high values, pop music did the same, and education also reinforced those parental values. Now in adulthood, the parents of Xers feel they can loosen the reins a bit and give their kids more freedom, more input, more choices than they were given. But that is precisely when the neighborhoods start to become less safe, the commercial radio and TV and music industries targeting children become more exploitive and coarse, and education relaxes its discipline. *Who saw all of this coming?*

Experiment # 4 – mobile society: America will become a mobile society just as Xers are born. As America's business model evolves from locally owned enterprises to national conglomerates, the parents of Xer kids will often *have* to advance their careers by accepting company promotions to other cities or states or nations. Not only that, as television now brings every corner of America right into the living rooms of all of its citizens, many parents of Xer children will leave their roots because they *want* to. They want to sample life in other cities and states. The lyrics of a popular Carole King song from the early '70s capture this newly mobile society:

"So far away...
Doesn't anybody stay in one place anymore?

It would be so fine to see your face at my door...
It doesn't help to know that you're so far away...."

And so, like no prior generation of American children, a significant number of Xer kids will be uprooted and come of age geographically separated from their relatives and friends, distanced from the family's roots. And these Xers will come of age attending fewer family reunions, fewer weddings of a-friend-of-their-next-door-neighbor's-sister-in-law, fewer funerals of your-great-uncle's-second-cousin-on-his-mother's-side. The cozy and nurturing cocoon of the American hometown and the extended family unit begins to unravel for this new generation of American children.

"A Nation at Risk" (1983)

So in this era of divorce, latchkey, time-starved career parents, a less clear message of right and wrong, and loss of the hometown roots, the classroom performance of this generation does indeed dip from that of earlier generations.

And in 1983, as the first Xers are graduating from high school, the landmark report *A Nation at Risk* describes "a rising tide of mediocrity (emerging from America's schools) that threatens our very future as a nation and as a people," adding "More and more young people emerge from high school ready neither for college nor work."

With that, Xer bashing begins: scathing news stories, editorial columns, and personal opinions down at the corner tavern about Xers being a lost generation, an underachieving generation...

... a slacker generation.

But *A Nation at Risk* also points out that the education system is letting Xer students down, describing "disturbing inadequacies in the way the educational process is conducted."

From this one part of their formative years experience come several strong and distinctive core values and beliefs. As with all other generations, some values are considered positive, some not so positive.

Independence
Self-reliance
Distance from Older Generations
Marriage is Disposable
Us against Them

Xers develop:

- a strong sense of independence and self-reliance;
- a noteworthy sense of distance from older generations that most Xers even today can't fully appreciate because theirs is the only childhood they know;
- a belief, with divorce by older people occurring all around them, that marriage must be something that is disposable;
- And, an attitude of *okay, looks like it's gonna be us against them; us Xers against those older people who are constantly criticizing us.*

Media Isolation

In addition to career moms, divorced parents, worka-holic parents, and that uprooting from extended family members, Gen X's sense of distance from older people is also the result of another phenomenon – a major pivot in American life – that is occurring for the first time in history, and it just happens to be occurring during the formative years of Gen X:

Media isolation.

In the 1970s and '80s, the number of radio stations in most American cities suddenly increases, as FM radio takes off. Lots of choices on the radio.

So American children no longer have to share one or two AM radio stations with their parents' and grandparents' generations, as prior generations had done in childhood; instead, Xers now have their very own stations, which program only to them and advertise only to them. *It's all about them.*

In the '80s, the same thing occurs with television as cable TV arrives, and Xers become the first children to have their very own TV channels that program and advertise only to them. *It's all about them.*

And with both Dad and Mom now enjoying career op-portunities, thanks to the women's movement, many American households – for the first time – can afford multiple TV sets. So many Xer kids come of age watching their favorite shows on TV set # 2 in room # 2, while Mom and Dad watch different shows on TV set # 1 in room # 1.

And so TV viewing becomes, for many Xer kids, a *solitary* experience or a peer-only experience, an isolating experience that separates them from older people.

So Xer kids miss the kind of typical multigenerational TV-viewing experience of February 9, 1964, February 16, 1964, and February 23, 1964.

The importance of these three consecutive Sunday nights is not just that every Boomer child who was old enough to hold a spoon was flopped on the living room floor watching the Beatles' three historic appearances on the Ed Sullivan show. The importance is that Mom and Dad, sitting behind the kids in the easy chairs, were also watching. And a couple miles away, Grandma and Grandpa were watching because in a four-channel universe, programming had to be multigenerational in its appeal. And Grandma and Grandpa knew that the act that followed the Beatles would be targeting *them.*

And the next day, and next week, and next family reunion, Boomer kids – and their parents and grandparents – had a television experience to share and discuss. And by doing so, Boomer kids learned just *another inch* of information about their elders, and elders learned another inch about Boomer kids, and so they drew closer together.

Xer kids, by having their own separate radio and TV channels, thus lose uncounted thousands of these little "inches" of connection to their elders. And so, beyond their control, they come of age more distanced from those elders.

Radio and television had always brought younger and older people together and strengthened intergenerational understanding and bonding. But now, in the '70s and '80s, these two media are pushing the generations apart.

A female Gen Xer, in a recent seminar audience, came up to me afterward and said, "Isn't it sad that I can actually remember *the one time* our whole family watched something together on TV? It was the 1984 Olympics."

Commercial radio and television
Race to the bottom

In addition to media *isolation*, Xers also are the first generation of kids who will come of age absorbing an all-out bombardment of vulgarity, violence, celebrity bashing, and sexual titillation from commercial radio and television and the music industry.

Beginning in the '70s and '80s, as the number of radio stations and TV channels sharply increases and competition for advertising dollars becomes brutal and desperate, some of those stations and channels instantly race to the bottom. I witness this from the inside. I'm working in major market radio when it begins in that medium, and I move to television when – a few years later – *that* medium becomes desperate.

Moderately talented or under-talented radio disc jockeys can't compete for ratings with the truly talented jocks in their market, most of whom are still clean-talking, informative, and upbeat personalities, as radio had always been. So in order to keep their jobs by increasing their own shows' ratings, they find easy ways to *shock* listeners into listening: cuss words, intimate sex talk, and – most widespread – celebrity bashing, which doesn't require much talent to pull off. And so shock jock radio enters American life, begun by desperate disc jockeys and approved by station executives who look the other way because it's getting ratings. *Instead of bringing out the best instincts in American listeners, let's increase our ratings by bringing out their worst instincts with shock radio.*

Same thing with television. Suddenly, dozens of channels need shows to air 24/7 but there is not enough true creative talent to go around, and not every show can win the ratings battle. Lesser-talented TV executives and show producers and writers and on-camera performers can't compete with the high-quality shows. Solution? Race to the bottom. Let's shock viewers into watching our show by giving them violence, vulgarity, and sex scenes like they've never seen. *Instead of bringing out the best instincts in American viewers, let's get ratings by bringing out their worst instincts with shock television.*

And it works! Howard Stern and other radio shock jocks earn ratings and fortunes. Ditto, shock television. And triple ditto, the unending bombardment of Gen X children with the sexually titillating images and coarse language of MTV's music videos and "reality" shows.

And there's more: it is during this time that commercial media begin *rewarding the bad guys.* Radio gives G. Gordon Liddy, the mastermind of the Watergate break-in, his own syndicated show. Crime pays! Women who have sexual affairs with married politicians or religious leaders become media darlings and cash in. Scandal pays! Do something bad? Book deal! Media executives figure that, in the crowded media landscape, a well-known "name," even if well-known for all the wrong reasons, can "cut through the clutter" and deliver revenues.

And a generation of American children – Xers – are passing through their important formative years during this era. Xers have never known any other media model. To Gen X, vulgarity and violence and sex and celebrity bashing and bad guys getting rewarded are *America*.

Trivialized and marginalized

The net effect of all this? Youth-targeted media *trivialize* Generation X by overwhelming them in childhood with the relentless message that fame and wealth and sex are what's *really* important, and our nation's leaders in government and business and education and religion exist to be bashed and mocked by media.

This trivialization delivers the inevitable consequence: in large part, because of the media message to them in childhood, Xers will enter adulthood *marginalized* to the outer edges of American life – less influential on, and critical to, those elements of life that *are* important. Instead of reading the main section of the daily newspaper and the weekly news magazines, Xers will make circulation and revenue successes of *People* and *Us Weekly* as those publications dish the celebrity gossip. They'll watch the cable shows that mock "the system" instead of the shows that earnestly try to explain and improve it. All of this comes from their formative years' experience with the commercial media, over which they had virtually no control. They were *kids*.

After a training seminar in one of the western states, I was taken to dinner by four Gen X women – in their late twenties to early thirties at the time – who work for the organization that hosted the seminar. At one point during our conversation, I asked them, "If you go to a Gen X party on a Saturday night, what does everybody talk about?" The answer, without hesitation: "Celebrities. J-Lo and Ben!" (Jennifer Lopez and Ben Affleck were the hot Hollywood couple at the time).

The Quarter-Life Crisis

I hadn't heard the term *quarer-life crisis* until 2004, when *Atlanta Journal-Constitution* reporter Don Fernandez called me for generational insights into a story the paper would headline, "Get-rich-fast ideal, celebrity culture lead twenty-somethings to frustration."

The quarter-life crisis refers to the negative influence – of MTV and other media – on coming-of-age Xers as they reach adulthood. This crisis is also summed up in a single line of dialogue in the 1999 Gen X-targeted movie *Fight Club*:

"We've all been raised on television to believe that, one day, we'd all be millionaires and movie gods and rock stars. But we won't. And we're slowly learning that fact. And we're very, very pissed off."

This is a fictitious line in a Hollywood movie (spoken by

Brad Pitt). But in this 2004 newspaper story, real-life Gen X comments repeat that sentiment:

Xer Cathy Stocker, then thirty-four, calls the relentless TV presentations of the luxuries and excesses of wealthy young adults the "American idolization of career expectations." Stocker runs the Web site quarterlifecrisis.com.

Xer Russell Tanton, then twenty-five, told the *Journal-Constitution*, "I don't think anyone was straight with people my age about how low our expectations actually should have been."

Xer Leslie Wright, then thirty-one, added, "You turn on the TV, and you see *The Apprentice*, the super-fab restaurants, the designer clothes. It's telling you that's what you should aim for. But I know that in twenty years, I won't have done anything better for the world."

As then twenty-eight-year-old Jason Shepherd told the *Journal-Constitution*, "Two years ago, there would not be a day when MTV was not on.... Now I can't remember the last time I watched it."

In this story, the quarter-life crisis is described by Xers themselves, as is their own wising up to the reality of adulthood and the emergence of a new generational attitude to judge their personal happiness by what they, not society, thinks of them. But it's not easy to shrug off the media influences – good and bad – of one's formative years.

Today in adulthood, as they enjoy greater control of their own lives than they did in childhood, Xers are beginning to find their footing. They're chalking up victories in their careers and family lives, beginning to make their positive mark on American life. It's looking more and more as if they'll overcome what some of those commercial media did to them during their formative years. If they do, it's likely they'll leave the *fringe* of American life, where the unique media messages of their childhood had pushed them, and wade in to life's main arena.

By the way, the younger Millennials are also absorbing that same media message that celebrity and wealth are what count. And as you'll read in their generation's chapters, a research study shows that *their top two goals in life are to be famous and rich.* And that has psychologists and sociologists very worried that Millennials are growing up to define themselves by what total strangers think of them.

Okay, back to Gen X's formative years....

X and Sex

The Silent Generation had come of age before the birth control pill and had to be careful about casual sex because of the fear of pregnancy. Boomers had come of age after the pill and before the HIV virus and so frolicked with sex, but nonetheless experienced a large number of unwanted pregnancies.

Ask Xers what comes to mind when they think of sex during their generation's formative years.

Condoms. Date rape. AIDS. Death.

The Computer Generation

Xers are the first generation to grow up with another brand new medium to go along with radio and TV: the revolutionary personal computer!

The very, very good news? Xers are developing a positive core value: a sense of pride that they are the computer generation. And they are. *TIME* magazine declared them so, with a cover story in 1982.

The downside is this: the new and exciting PC has one drawback during the formative years of most Xers. The Internet is not yet attached to it. This box is not yet connected to other human beings, as it will be for younger Millennials. And so the computer becomes still one more *isolating* activity, as radio and TV have just become. As *New York Times* reporter James Fallows wrote in 2006, in a story contrasting how *Millennials* are nowadays growing up with constant connectedness to other human beings, "In the beginning, personal computers were for loners."

So in contrast to prior generations and now the Millennials, many Xer children are spending more time in individual and solitary and peer-only pursuits and less time in the presence of parents and other adults.

And this part of their formative years' experience will mold core values and attitudes that will influence Xers' career choices, lifestyle preferences, and consumer decisions for a lifetime.

A sedentary generation – or not?

Gen X is an interesting paradox when it comes to the issue of fitness and nutrition.

Xers are the first generation in history to *come of age* with fitness and nutrition as front-page topics, not to mention all those female sports opportunities in their schools (more on that in a minute).

But they also come of age sedentary, sitting or standing for hours in front of these new and seductive video games and personal computers, whose lure is nothing short of phenomenal. Prior generations had raced outdoors after school, after dinner, and on weekends and burned off the calories. Xers race to the video game or PC and sit.

They're also the first generation of school kids to eat lunches in cafeterias that now offer greasy and fatty burgers, fries, and pizza, and candy bars and sugary soft drinks every single day instead of the nutritionally balanced (but not especially *yummy*) plate lunches older generations had eaten in their youth.

And to compound the obesity threat, the time-starved, dual-career parents of Xers succumb more and more to drive-through fast food for the family. And during Xers' formative years, most fast-food chains are not yet offering a lot of healthier alternatives to their mainstay burger/fries/cola menu.

So, a generation that could've become America's most physically fit instead becomes – pretty much beyond its control – the leading edge of a child obesity epidemic that continues today and is even worse with the younger Millennials.

I've presented Generational Marketing Strategy at two national conferences of the Produce Marketing Association, whose research shows that older Americans eat more fruits and vegetables than Xers do. The PMA is exploring strategies to get Xers and Millennials to purchase more fresh produce, not only for themselves but also for their Millennial children. One of the problems is time poorness, which forces many Xers – and Boomers – to make the obligatory trip to the supermarket as *infrequently* as they possibly can. And as the interim between trips grows longer, uneaten produce often goes "bad" before the next trip, so Xers and Boomers and their children frequently go a few days – or more – with no fresh produce in the house. The produce industry is exploring ways to extend the shelf life of its fruits and veggies, as well as looking into new methods to get fresh produce to busy Xers and Boomers more conveniently than it currently does. Xers and Boomers, do you need *home delivery* of fresh produce? Or, do you need it to be made available in locations besides the supermarket? What if your employer invested in a modest produce "store" in the workplace so you could buy it as you leave work for the day?

Premature wealth
Refined tastes
Appreciation of Mom & Dad

A significant number of Xers also come of age experiencing what sociologists call "premature wealth."

In part because so many households now have dual incomes, in part because so many of those divorced parents feel guilty, and in part because many concerned grandparents are witnessing the struggle their Xer grandkids are experiencing and want to do something – *anything* – to help them through this difficult passage, many Xers go through their formative years being showered with expensive *stuff*.

Designer-label clothing, $150 sneakers, their own TV sets, their own stereos, their own telephones, their own computers, and often their own unshared bedrooms. And in many cases their own cars, which beginning in the 1980s forces many high schools nationwide to find extra acreage in order to create *student* parking lots.

And this part of their formative years creates a generational consumer value of refined and expensive tastes. *Xers know quality.* And when they reach adulthood, to the greatest extent that their incomes permit, Xers will demand quality in the goods and services they purchase.

But there's a flip side to this premature wealth too. Here's what a 36-year-old Gen X male e-mailed to me after hearing my recent Gen X presentation in St. Petersburg, Florida:

"If we are the 'divorce' generation," he wrote, "we are also the original 'Deadbeat Dad' generation. My dad still owes my mom money. What is it like to wear a $150 pair of shoes? I have no idea."

But on another matter, a lot of Xers also say this:

Maybe Mom and Dad weren't around as much I would've liked during my childhood, but I do appreciate all of their hard work for me. I know how hard they worked.

African-American Xers
black/white gap shrinking
Post-civil rights
Careers
Suburbs

The formative years' experiences of African-American Xers are closer to those of white Xers than in any prior generation – the gap is getting smaller – but there are some differences.

Black Xers are the first generation of children to come of age after the Civil Rights Movement of the '60s and early '70s, and the positive changes they see are exciting and happening quickly!

Suddenly, African-Americans are no longer one big "monolith," one big homogeneous group with similar jobs, similar incomes, residing in similar neighborhoods, living similar lives.

Instead, that monolith is now breaking up:

- a significant number of blacks are landing leadership jobs, white-collar jobs, different and better jobs than before;
- some are moving from the inner cities to the previously all-white suburbs;
- black Xer kids now see people of color in high-visibility

jobs, as elected officials, news anchors and reporters, doctors and lawyers and professionals in other fields, and they see them flourishing more than ever in sport and entertainment;

- school busing occurs during the formative years of Gen X and intermingles young black and white kids more thoroughly than America had ever done before; and although it isn't always easy, Gen X blacks and Gen X whites learn more about each other than any prior generation of American kids.

Anecdote: in the early 1990s, I produced and hosted a half-hour television special for the ABC affiliate in Columbus, Ohio. It was a live-audience talk show about Gen X, with a studio audience of fifty-five Gen X high school juniors and seniors who would've been born in the late 1970s. The name of this TV Special was *Sneakers* (not to be confused with the Robert Redford movie of the same name, which came out soon after).

We taped for a couple of hours in order to edit the footage into a tight thirty-minute finished show. We talked about all-things-Gen X, and at one point deep into the taping, I threw this one out to them:

"Are you racists?"

Their response, a one-word *chorus,* was the most passionate response we captured during the entire taping.

"No!"

One white 17-year-old Gen X boy stood and said with pride, "In fact, I think we're the first generation to *come of age* as a non-racist generation." Fifty-four other heads, a mixed-race audience by design, heartily nodded in agreement.

Gen Xers develop core values of being an especially inclusive, nonjudgmental generation.

The Cosby Show
1984 to 1992

As Xer children come of age, *The Cosby Show* finally presents – to both black and white viewers, thanks to the color-blind appeal of star Bill Cosby and its talented cast – an African-American family with parents who are happily married and professionally successful. As one African-American female newspaper reporter would tell me years later, for a lot of black Xer kids with only one parent, this show becomes an influential model of an intact and happy and successful African-American family.

A Different World
1987 to 1993

And the TV show *A Different World* has a similar impact, presenting a college education as an attainable opportunity for Xer blacks.

Doctor King

And on January 20, 1986, right in the middle of Gen X's formative years, Congress approves legislation creating a national holiday in honor of Martin Luther King, Jr.

Crack

But amid all of this sudden optimism for African-Americans, the formative years of Xer blacks are also dotted by some negatives, among them the horrible impact of crack cocaine, which begins ravaging black (and white) communities in the early '80s and grows into a full-blown monster by the end of the decade.

Strong Female Generation; Males Seek Identity

In adulthood, and this will usually ignite a lively discussion at a Gen X party, Xers have emerged as an especially confident and assertive female generation, while many Gen X males – the evidence is unmistakable – are still kind of searching for their identity, for their masculinity, for their focus.

And marketers are playing to this gender dynamic in a very big way.

Here's what it's all about:

- During this generation's formative years of the '70s, '80s, and '90s, young Gen X girls are coming of age soaking up the full force of the feminist message that is all around them, in the classroom and the living room. They hear it from Mom and Dad, and from their educators: *there are no limits. You can do what you want to do, be what you want to be, go where you want to go. Go ahead and dream your biggest dream!* Girls' confidence? Up!

- This is when the education industry, for the first time, begins to place a special focus on girl-friendly education. The Girl Project (1973), initially designed to eliminate girls' traditional weaknesses in math and science, does so much more! Gen X females methodically surpass the classroom performance of the boys in elementary school and later in the nation's college classrooms, when in the early 1990s those Gen X women become the first to surpass the men in virtually every academic measurement. The girls' confidence grows even more; the boy's confidence takes another hit.

- In 1972, just as the leading edge of Gen X is entering its school years, Congress passes Title IX, the landmark legislation that forces American schools and colleges to offer equal opportunities for boys and girls in sport. So a good number of Xer boys go through their school years seeing some of their sports reduced – or cut altogether – to make budgetary room for the girls, while Xer girls see their athletic opportunities swiftly expand. Thirty years later, in the early 2000s, the TV show *60 Minutes* aired a segment on Title IX, asking now-adult Gen Xers to reflect upon the impact of this legislation on their lives. One Xer woman spoke for her entire generation when she said, *"We know we're the Lucky Title 9 Babies."*

- Also during Gen X's formative years, and this would be The Big One in this gender dynamic, the nation's suddenly busy divorce courts are overwhelmingly awarding child custody to Mom, not Dad, *not back then.*

So millions of Xer boys will try to climb to manhood while living in a female-supervised home, where they might see Dad only every other weekend, if that. And if one Gen X boy has just one sister, then – yikes! – he is also growing up in a female-*dominated* household!

Fight Club

This frustration with female dominance shows up in a 1999 movie about the disillusioned Gen X male in early adulthood. It's entitled *Fight Club*.

In the early scenes of this film, two bewildered Gen X guys – portrayed by actors Brad Pitt and Edward Norton – are sitting together in a crummy bar in a crummy section of town, reflecting on their discouragement with adulthood and trying to figure out this frilly, feminine, pro-girl era in which they were raised.

At one point, Brad Pitt asks Edward Norton, "Do you know what a duvet is??"

Norton answers matter-of-factly, "Yeah, a duvet is a comforter."

In disgust, Pitt says it for all Gen X men, "What are guys like us doing, *knowing what a duvet is.*"

DeGreve Oil Change

That formative years' experience helps to explain a print ad that the *Quad-City Times* created for one of its clients,

DeGreve Oil Change, a chain of seven oil-and-lube shops in the greater Davenport, Iowa, market.

Owner John DeGreve attended my half-day presentation on Generational Marketing and Advertising Strategy, sponsored by the *Times*. A week later, interested in learning more, Mr. DeGreve, along with the newspaper's account rep and graphic artist, sat down with me for a one-hour brainstorming session in the *Times'* conference room.

According to Mr. DeGreve and his industry's own research, G.I. and Silent and Boomer men are very consistent at changing the oil in their vehicles on a regular schedule. Xer guys are *not!* Why? How?

We arrived at this explanation: G.I. and Silent and Boomer boys had come of age when American dads changed their own oil in the garage or driveway. Not always an easy task, so it was a memorable ritual. Young boys hung around Dad to watch and learn, and help Dad a little. They also heard Dad preach, "When you learn to drive and someday own your own car, remember – you change the oil regularly!" The preaching stuck. And so in adulthood, they, too, change the oil regularly.

But: (1) Xer boys came of age with dual-career, time-starved parents who often didn't have the time to change the oil themselves but did have the money to drive the car to the quick-change oil-and-lube stores; (2) because of the high divorce rate, many Gen X boys saw Dad only every other weekend, if that; and (3) Xer boys had a generation of parents who didn't want to be as "preachy" as their own parents had been with them. So the boyhood ritual of Dad's oil change and Dad's constant reminder – "you change the oil regularly!" – were lost as American life evolved.

So in our brainstorming session, I mentioned, "You know, it's almost as if fathers need to have *two talks* with their coming-of-age sons. One talk is the birds-and-bees discussion about sex. And the other talk is 'you change the oil regularly!'"

The print ad, which we conceived after only about fifteen minutes of conversation, shows a Boomer father standing outdoors in front of the family car with his arm around his now adult Gen X son, smiling as he looks at him and says, "Son, it's time we had *the talk*. If you don't keep it properly lubricated, it won't last very long." And, at the bottom of the ad, "Things my father never told me."

Marketing to GenX women

So, how do marketers go after those strong Gen X women??

With TV commercials like Soft 'n Dry deodorant, which shows an Xer woman kickboxing. Or a fabric softener showing an Xer woman practicing karate.

Best Buy

Or the retail electronics chain Best Buy producing a recent fantasy concept for a TV spot promoting its big-screen TV sets. The commercial shows a Gen X married couple in street clothes but wearing skates and magically competing in a professional ice hockey game! The husband controls the puck. Just as he gets slammed to the boards by an opponent, he yells "Honey!" and passes the puck cross-ice to his Title IX Gen X wife, who superhumanly leaps over a fallen player while maintaining control of the puck, and then wins the game with a long slap shot just as time expires. Husband and wife then skate to the edge of the ice, where – again, magically – they're now standing inside a Best Buy store, looking at a big-screen TV set.

This spot shatters three stereotypes. First, Gen X women no longer leave the big electronics purchasing decisions to their husbands; it's no longer a "man's" job. Second, the athletic, confident Title IX Gen X woman has the athletic skills and confidence to score the winning goal in a hockey game in which all other competitors are men. And third, it shows the "new" American husband: the Gen X husband who trusts his wife's consumer wisdom and physical skills. Excellent generational messaging to Xers, who take pride in their generational core value of marriage "between equals."

Secret deodorant

A recent Secret deodorant television spot celebrates the athletic, independent, assertive Gen X female but also pokes lighthearted fun at the emasculated Gen X guy who tried to go from boyhood to manhood during the era of the Surging Female. The gender roles are completely reversed in this spot.

As the spot begins, we see a car with a flat tire parked alongside a busy highway. A second car pulls off the road behind it. Stepping out of Car # 2 is gorgeous and athletically toned Gen X wife in a dress and heels. Coming out of Car # 1 to meet her is her frazzled and effeminate Gen X husband, who is exasperated and confused, assuming the traditional stereotype of the helpless *female*. He tells his wife:

"Thank god you came! Look, I know you had that thing tonight, but I didn't know what else to do. I mean, cars were whizzing by, and I think my cell's almost dead, and I – "

Title IX wife calmly holds up her hand to stop his nervous blather and quietly asks, "Where's the spare?"

Gen X husband looks at her, bewildered. "The spare *what?*"

She swiftly changes the tire, brushes the dirt from her hands, smiles, says "Okay – all set!" As she strides confidently back to her car, her emasculated and dumbfounded husband stares blankly down at the newly installed tire and mutters, "Good, I'll take it from here." The tagline at the end of the spot?

"Secret: Strong Enough for a Woman."

Years earlier, the tagline had been, "Secret: Strong Enough for a Man, but Gentle Enough for a Woman." But not now. Not with these confident and assertive Title IX women.

Lowe's and Home Depot
Pursuing Xer and Boomer women
Store/Web site/catalog redesign
DIY workshops

The nation's two largest home-improvement chains, Lowe's and Home Depot, recently launched competitive marketing campaigns in pursuit of Xer and Boomer women, who, according to both companies' research, are willing to tackle the *big* home-improvement jobs around the house. In many cases, these two confident generations of women *want* to take on these projects. In other cases, with so many of them living on their own, they *must.*

So both Lowe's and Home Depot made changes, such as renovating their stores and redesigning their Web sites and catalogs to be more female friendly. One of these chains found that its aisles were too narrow, that female shoppers were experiencing what the research describes as "butt brush": as they squeezed past each other sideways in the narrow aisles, women's butts brushed each other. So aisles were widened.

These two retailers also began offering periodic do-it-yourself training sessions right in their stores. After attending a recent seminar in Oregon, an audience member who works for one of these chains said his store's recent Saturday morning session had attracted about eighty percent female DIY wannabes.

Generational strategy can help to guide store planning and design: space planning, lighting, fixturing, color palette, signage, merchandising, and more.

Let's take a quick side trip from our story of the strong Gen X female, while we're on the subject of facility planning. A couple of examples:

Generationally strategized buildings and facilities

There is currently a boom in college campus construction. New dorms, student centers, recreation facilities. The current-day question is simply this: what does the Millennial Generation college student want and need in physical facilities?

For example: unlike self-focused Gen Xers who often prefer to work alone, Millennials – as you'll read – are much more a team-focused, "we" generation. Group structure is comfortable to "Mils." Might influence the floor plan.

I recently met with one of the nation's more prominent firms in office building architecture, which is conducting generationally designed research studies instead of merely demographic studies to determine what Boomer and Xer and Millennial employees prefer and need in the workplace of the future. Open spaces? Walled cubicles? Traditional enclosed offices? What about the design and placement of the company's conference rooms and common spaces? And what about the ergonomic needs of the generations, regarding noise suppression (according to an audiologist client, twenty million Americans have significantly impaired hearing, and Xers and Millennials – from too many loud concerts and too much childhood use of music headsets that inject the audio right into your ear from pointblank range – will probably suffer hearing loss at an earlier age and in bigger numbers than prior generations), cubicle and desk and chair design

(Millennials are America's most obese generation of children ever; the research blames poor nutrition habits and their sedentary, sit-at-the-computer lives), and so on.

Okay, back to our strong Gen X female.

All of this generational marketing – the Secret deodorant flat tire commercial, Best Buy's hockey spot, the Lowe's and Home Depot strategies, and many other case studies – is nothing more than the inevitable by-product of Gen X's unique formative years' experiences with girl-friendly education, Title IX legislation, boy's discouragement, and the women's movement.

If we understand a generation's unique formative years, we can then make sense of the unique generational core values that arose from those formative years. Armed with that powerful knowledge, we can then "message" to those core values in the marketplace and workplace. And, in the *living room* with our own families, as we understand each other even *more* completely.

"Restore Your Manhood"

How about messaging to these emasculated GenX men?

A TV commercial by Hummer vehicles shows two Xer guys standing side by side at adjacent supermarket checkout counters. One guy is buying a huge brick of tofu, while the other guy is buying slabs of red-meat ribs. They look at each other's groceries on the conveyor belt. Tofu guy is embarrassed. Red-meat guy gives Tofu guy a quick look of pity. Then Tofu guy glances away and notices a picture of a Hummer on the store's magazine rack. He swiftly leaves the supermarket, drives to the Hummer dealership, buys one, and as he drives away the on-screen written slogan says it all for Gen X males: "Restore Your Manhood."

Marketing to Gen X men
Female denigration
TV programming
Commercials
Music
Video games

Now it gets a little ugly.

Here's how other corners of the American marketplace have responded to what some marketers perceive – whether they're right or wrong – to be the Gen X male's formative years' frustration with that female dominance.

Commercial television and radio (as distinguished from *public* television and radio) have responded to this attitude with what's considered to be *female-denigrating* programming: Howard Stern, Jerry Springer, The Man Show, and others, which target – at least in part – Xer men and which have consistently presented Gen X women as little more than sexual slabs of meat, and usually without much brainpower.

Beer commercials: Coors used big-breasted females jumping on a trampoline. The Coors Twins!

"Another round of raunch"

Miller Beer launched its infamous "catfight" series of commercials. A commentary in *Ad Age* magazine, headlined "Another round of raunch," describes this series this way: "Miller Brewing Co. will take raunchy marketing to a new extreme in the coming months...."

Many music videos and lyrics, especially beginning with early '90s rap, deliver what many feel is that same kind of female denigration, by using video images and song lyrics that relentlessly present women as sex instruments. More than one Xer woman has told me the female denigration in music also shows up in heavy metal from the '80s.

And the video-game industry is under similar attack. A hot seller in recent years has been the video game called *Grand Theft Auto*, one early version of which awards points to players who have sex with a prostitute in a car, then push her out of the car and onto the ground and kick and shoot her to death.

The television show *60 Minutes* aired a segment on *Grand Theft Auto*. Its investigative team set up in a large department store's video game department during the holiday season and videotaped mothers grabbing *Grand Theft Auto* from the shelves, taking it to the checkout counter, and paying for it. Then *60 Minutes* intercepted those mothers as they were leaving the store. The conversations went something like this:

(*60 Minutes*): "Hi, what did you just buy?"
(American mother): "Oh, a video game for my son."
"How old is he?"

"Nine (or thirteen, or eleven)."

"Wha'd ya buy?"

"Grand Theft Auto."

"Have you seen it?"

"No, it was just on my son's Christmas list, so I bought it."

"Wanna come over to our table and take a quick look?"

"Sure."

One by one, these mothers watched in horror at what they had just purchased for their sons.

Unimpressed with authority
Cynical towards older generations
Distrustful of major institutions
Disempowerment
Disengagement

Because of what's going in the adult world during their formative years, both male and female Xers are developing another set of core values, and in many cases these values are toughening them in the right way for their own adulthood. Xers are growing up to be:

- rather unimpressed with authority;
- cynical towards older generations;
- distrustful of major institutions;
- and, in 180-degree contrast to all of the other living generations, Xers also are developing a deep core value of disempowerment. And with that sense of disempowerment comes its inevitable twin value: disengagement.

Think about it:

Gen X and government

All around them as they come of age in the '70s and '80s
and '90s, Xers see one adult institution after another fail
to deliver on its promise. They see the leaders of those
institutions lying, cheating, breaking the law, and *exploiting* Americans rather than *serving* them. Take the biggest
institution of all: government.

Ask a G.I. what "government" meant to them in their formative years and they'll recall the FDR administration,
which heroically held the nation together and ultimately
led it out of the Great Depression and then to victory
in WW II. Ask Silents, and they'll tell you about "their
generation's" President Eisenhower, who presided over a
joyous, economically surging, safe, and cohesive America
after World War II. First-Wave Boomers will remember
a charismatic presidential candidate who, at a speech
at the University of Michigan, inspired the creation of
the Peace Corps and who later promised the world that
America would safely land a man on the moon before
the end of the decade – *and we did.*

But it starts to unravel with Second-Wave Boomers and
even more so with Xers.

Here's "government" to Gen X kids coming of age in the
'70s, '80s, and '90s:

- In 1973, as the first Xers turn eight, they learn that
  the vice president of their country just resigned in
  scandal.
- In 1974, as they turn nine, young Xers learn the president of their country just resigned in scandal.

- In 1975, as they turn ten, they learn their government just quit a war.
- In 1979, as they turn fourteen, they join CBS News anchor Walter Cronkite and all Americans in a nationwide count of 444 days of Americans held hopelessly hostage by terrorists in Iran.
- In 1980, as they turn fifteen, they witness the national embarrassment of a failed attempt by their government to rescue those hostages.
- From 1983 to 1988, right in the middle of their generation's formative years, Xer kids see the daily playing out on television of the Iran-Contra scandal.
- On January 28, 1986, just about every Xer – all these years later – still remembers where he or she was when the space shuttle Challenger exploded, because in 1986 every level of American classroom – from kindergarten to college senior – was filled by Xers and that was the space launch that had taken along its first-ever school teacher, so students everywhere were tuned in and witnessed the explosion "live" only a couple of minutes after launch, when ground-based TV cameras still had the spaceship in focus.
- And in the 1990s, it is the impeachment of President Clinton over the Paula Jones and Monica Lewinsky sex allegations and scandals, in which the president confesses that he "misled" Americans in his sworn testimony about his sexual improprieties.
- And finally, Xer kids see the beginning of political campaigns that abandon the notion of using campaign advertising to explain a candidate's qualifications and positions to voters and, instead, use the advertising to launch unprecedented dirty-tricks campaigning and attack ads on the opponent. Sleaze campaigning overruns the democratic process.

And these kinds of one-after-the-other formative years' events tend to solidify in Gen X the understandable core values of *distrust* of government and, with it, *disinterest* in government. And to this day, that core value shows up with Xers' well-documented lack of interest in following the *hard news* of the day and a lack of interest in *voting in elections.*

I consult dozens of television stations and newspapers on generational strategy because media research documents that Gen X is not watching local TV news, network TV news, and they're not reading the main section – which traditionally has presented the important government and big-business news – of their daily newspapers in the same high percentages that prior generations had done at that age. Even younger Millennials are more plugged-in to the hard news than Gen X.

This is a crisis for the news industry because Xers are currently a major target of advertiser spending, and the news department has historically been the big money-maker for local TV stations, the big opportunity for the major TV networks to distinguish their brand, and the absolute lifeblood, naturally, of newspapers.

The Wall Street Journal crafted an advertising campaign to enhance readership and circulation amongst Gen Xers. Rather than try to convert Xers from disengaged to engaged with a heavy-handed message, the print ads instead acknowledge this generation's cynicism while simply offering its product as a path to empowerment and engagement.

Creatively, each ad shows a photograph of a Gen Xer reading the WSJ, while the copy includes a sentence in which one cynical word or phrase is crossed out in favor of a more optimistic one.

One ad shows a young Xer professional sitting in an airplane seat, reading the WSJ. The copy reads: "My boss is ~~impossible~~ a sitting duck."

Another shows an Xer female at her breakfast table, sipping coffee, and reading the WSJ. Copy: "The boys' club keeps me ~~down~~ fighting."

Another shows a Gen X guy sitting in his small and cluttered cubicle: "My cubicle is a ~~black hole~~ launch pad."

And there were other variations on this same theme. This is good generation-specific messaging by *The Wall Street Journal*, acknowledging the unique core values that emerged from the unique formative years of an American generation.

And about Gen X's low participation rates as voters:

After I had presented multiple training sessions on Generational Newspaper Strategy to staffers of *The Columbus* (OH) *Dispatch*, its research department got curious and reviewed voting data from the 2004 general elections. What it found is surely symptomatic of the entire nation: Xers, then aged twenty-three to thirty-nine, were out-voted by older Silents and Boomers *and even the younger Millennials* as a percentage of registered voters who actually voted.

Compared to other generations, Gen Xers have thus far been significantly unplugged from government and the democratic process. *Disempowerment* and *disengagement.* A direct and predictable consequence of the times of their unique formative years.

An aside to G.I.s, Silents, Boomers, and Millennials: if you had been born when Xers were born and had come of age witnessing the same government they witnessed, you would be unplugged, distrustful, and disinterested too. We have virtually no control over the year we're born. So we also have no control over the unique times and teachings that will occur during our formative years and will mold our generation's unique and lifelong core values. Same with you, Xers: if you had been born in 1955, you would be carrying the core values of Boomers.

When we all acknowledge this fundamental truth, we suddenly find ourselves making peace with the different values and attitudes of the other generations, and we then start *rooting* for those other generations to find their own success and happiness in life, *given the hand they were dealt in childhood*. And we hope they'll understand *our* generations' unique values and start rooting for us too. And by embracing that outlook, America's generation gaps begin to shrink.

Gen X and big business

Not only do Xers come of age distrustful of, and disinterested in, government, but they also have the same experience with another major American institution, big business.

In 1973 and 1974, the oldest Xer children are age eight and nine when they learn that an oil embargo by a few obscure nations on the other side of the planet is bringing their America, supposedly the world's economic superpower, to its knees.

And throughout their formative years, many Xers will see their fathers and mothers laid off their jobs in massive numbers, despite their good hard work and loyalty to their employer, as America enters a lengthy period of corporate downsizing, rightsizing, consolidation, outsourcing, and all those other polite euphemisms for losing one's job because of industry shifts, incompetent management, or cost cutting.

And the news media will document how many of the bosses of their mothers and fathers are receiving handsome bonuses and pay raises in return for slashing those jobs, because the bosses' cost cutting has driven up the price of their public companies' stocks and pleased shareholders.

During the formative years of Gen X, history will document that the rich will get much richer, often at the expense of middle-class Americans, who take a beating during the '70s, '80s, '90s, and into the 2000s.

And these kinds of events mold Gen X core values of:

(1) a pretty healthy distrust of employers;

(2) a strong belief amongst Xers that they must look out for themselves when they enter the workplace because two-way loyalty between boss and employee is apparently dead;

(3) and a hardened Gen X attitude of *I'll be darned if I'm going to pledge blind loyalty to a company and then get blindsided with a layoff like Dad and Mom did.*

And Xers experience similar formative years' disappointments with other major American institutions:

- High-profile religious televangelists of the era go to prison for fraud (Jim Bakker) or confess to sin (Jimmy Swaggart).

- And it's during the formative years of Gen X kids that their sports heroes begin cheating, in noteworthy numbers, by taking performance-enhancing drugs. Not only that, because of a court ruling in the early '70s permitting "free agency," hometown pro-sports heroes suddenly may now switch teams in order to make more money. That's why athletes suddenly become millionaires, and it's also why Xers become America's first kids to have their hearts broken and their hero worship rebuffed when their favorite Cincinnati Red or Dallas Cowboy or Milwaukee Buc becomes, overnight, a Philadelphia Philly, Minnesota Viking, or Los Angeles Laker.

Gen X and disempowerment

So in this new culture, Xers come of age with a core value of disempowerment – a sense of powerlessness to do anything about all these major negative things swirling all around them during their youth:

- *My parents are divorcing and I can't do anything about it.* Or,

- *My parents are happily married, but my best friend's parents are divorcing and I can't do anything to help my hurting friend.*
- *My dad got laid off and I can't do anything about it.*
- *My career-driven mom accepted a transfer and is moving us a long distance from my friends, and I can't do anything about it.*
- *My country's leaders and heroes are lying and cheating and failing, and I can't do anything about it.*
- *My radio stations and TV channels are exploiting and trivializing me, instead of serving me, and I can't do anything about it.*

Reality Bites

This distrust of older generations and this sense of disempowerment are vividly presented in a 1994 Xer movie that is all about Gen Xers' life passage from college into an unfriendly adult world and job market. It's entitled *Reality Bites.*

And the movie begins with a graduation speech by an Xer valedictorian portrayed by the actress Winona Ryder who, in her valedictory address to her fellow Gen X graduating students, says this:

"And they wonder why those of us in our twenties refuse to work an eighty-hour week just so we can afford to buy their BMWs, why we aren't interested in the counterculture they invented…. But the question remains, what are we going to do now? How can we repair all the damage we inherited? Fellow graduates, the answer is simple. The answer is, I don't know."

I presented Generational Workforce Diversity to several

hundred California Professional Firefighters at their annual conference in Palm Springs. Afterward, a Gen X female firefighter came up and asked, "Could you see me sitting in the back row?" (I couldn't; the big hotel banquet room was darkened so the audience could more clearly view my PowerPoint slides). "Well, when you were walking through our generation's formative years, and I remembered my own pain, I started to cry, and I felt embarrassed. I looked up and down my row to see if anybody saw me, and that's when I saw two other Gen Xers teared up too."

Not too long ago, I watched a VH1 television documentary about grunge rocker Curt Cobain, whose cynical and defeatist song "Smells Like Teen Spirit" became a Gen X anthem in the early '90s as it reflected on this generation's formative years: "It's fun to lose... I feel stupid and contagious... with the lights out, it's less dangerous... oh well, whatever, never mind."

On that show, a reporter for one of the music industry magazines summed up the formative years of Gen X: "People didn't realize how badly kids were hurting."

The light at the end of the tunnel

Now, let's wrap a ribbon around those formative years' times and teachings and look at Xers today.

And you'll find that many *positive* beliefs and *positive* values have come out of those comparatively difficult childhood years.

No ideology
Pragmatic
Make marriage work
Be there for children
Work hard, make money
Not "joiners"

- Gen X is not a generation of any sweeping ideology or idealism. They do not claim a long list of universal causes; they've been too preoccupied trying to survive. So their attitude towards life tends to be one of pragmatism: *It's up to me. I have to take care of myself. Feet on the ground. I'll do what it takes in life to get things done, one decision at a time.*

- Xers are especially eager to make their marriages work and to *be there* for their own children because, in their formative years, such a large number of them experienced the opposite. A headline in the newspaper *USA Today* labels Gen X the "family-first generation." But it's not working out perfectly. They are divorcing in significant numbers.

- And in their careers, Xers want to work hard. They want to make money and be successful. Some of them just want to do the work differently from the ways it's been done before.

- Gen X is not, thus far, a generation of "joiners." And the impact is about to be profound. They are not joining local civic groups like the Lions and Rotary Clubs, and they're not joining professional trade associations, military veterans organizations, and other established volunteer and service organizations. The one noteworthy exception? Xer *parents* are more likely to participate if it involves their children. I present training sessions focusing on this single issue, as organizations such as American Society of Association Executives, Veterans of Foreign Wars, Texas Society of Certified Public Accountants, Tennessee Dental Association, and dozens of similar member and volunteer organizations ask the same question: *how can we get Gen Xers to join this organization, which is meant to benefit them?!*

Parenting versus career

The women of Gen X are especially sensitive to the career-versus-motherhood balancing act. A significant number of them, and a growing number of Xer dads, are ruling out all-consuming careers in order to be there for their children, especially during their kids' preschool years. Many employers are trying to accommodate this family-first core value with more generous maternity/paternity leave programs, telecommuting, and other innovations.

With their husbands, many Xer mothers are choosing the financial sacrifice of suspending one income in order to accommodate that core value of their generation: *I'm gonna be there for my kid.* Many other Xer parents would like to do this, but simply can't afford to.

And with that same value in mind, Xers might be more hesitant than prior generations to accept job offers or promotions that would uproot their families and move them to some distant city. And careers that include heavy overnight travel are sometimes a deal breaker with Xer parents.

The National Parent Teacher Association is advertising to this family-first core value:

A few years ago, the National PTA began running a print ad in the annual NASCAR Guide, the glossy magazine sold at NASCAR races and in the NASCAR mall stores. The ad simply encourages Gen X dads to join the PTA.

And it worked. The PTA chapters around the country report that membership among Gen X dads is up.

Self-focused
Peer-focused

Gen Xers are more self-focused and peer-focused than the other generations.

They grew up with their own radio stations and TV channels talking only to them, and they shared less time and daily conversation with older generations, so if it's not about them and for them, they might lose interest.

Nowhere is that more evident than in the newspaper industry where, in the early 2000s, a number of major-market dailies began publishing separate weekly tabloids dedicated to Gen X. The design, layout, graphics, editorial, and advertising content, and the staffs that produce them, were Gen X.

Not only that, daily newspapers – knowing that Xers are strongly interested in celebrities and celebrity gossip (think *People* magazine) – are now moving celebrity "fluff" – celebrity birthdays, celebrity scandal, celebrity couples news – to their main sections, trying to connect with this generation.

Xers like products, marketing, and advertising that embrace such Xer core values and attitudes as these:

- Attitude! Attitude! Attitude!
- Edgy.
- Cynical.
- Fun.
- Retro.
- After-Sale Warranty.

Xers possess attitude, love attitude, celebrate attitude. When messaging to them, load up with attitude.

They like messaging that's a bit edgy, a bit cynical. They like humor and fun in the marketing and advertising that targets them. Xers also love "retro" references to their youth. Retro to GenX is the 1970s, '80s, and '90s.

And because Xers came of age with all of those major institutions breaking their promises on a regular basis, they're concerned – especially with their major purchases – about the after-sale assurance. *If I buy this house/car/ refrigerator from you today and something goes wrong with it six months from now, are you gonna be there for me?*

General Motors delivers this entire list of Xer hot buttons in a single thirty-second commercial for its Chevy Cavalier:

We see a Cavalier parked in a big asphalt parking lot next to a long earthen levy. No other cars or people in sight.

Inside the car, Gen X Guy is stretched out in the driver's seat, singing along with the radio to "Bye-bye, Miss American Pie, drove my Chevy to the levy...." Outside the car, clearly bored and waiting impatiently for him, Gen X Girlfriend sits on the ground. The song ends. Smug and satisfied Gen X Guy crawls out of the car and orders his Girlfriend "Okay, let's go." She drearily gets up, joins him, and together they slowly shuffle off for a walk, as the female voiceover says, "Until the very end, we'll be there."

Lots of attitude in this spot. The spot is edgy, cynical, retro (music from the '70s), fun, and the tagline delivers the after-sale assurance: "Until the very end, we'll be there."

Very Gen X.

Here's one that missed the mark but still landed gloriously on its feet:

The Chrysler PT Cruiser.

As *The Wall Street Journal* wrote: "The PT Cruiser: designed for Gen X, but it was Boomers who bit."

Seemed like it should've worked with Xers; seemed to hit all of their hot buttons: the PT Cruiser is loaded with attitude. It's edgy, fun, and magnificently retro. But to Xers, "retro" means the 1970s and '80s and '90s, and the PT Cruiser is retro back to panel trucks and autos from the 1940s!! Oops, missed by thirty years!

But...

By about its second or third year on the market, and according to auto industry researcher R.L. Polk, the average driver profile of the PT Cruiser was a fifty-one-year-old Boomer male! The Boomers, old enough to remember that car design from their very early childhood, went wild for the PT Cruiser, which not only enhanced Chrysler revenues but also "grew Chrysler young" and helped to erase its "old people's car" image that Boomers had previously given it.

How did Chrysler seize the moment even more? By promptly adding two options on the PT Cruiser that nostalgically reminded Boomers of their youth: flame paint jobs (popular with "street rods" in the '50s) and fake wood grain paneling on the sides (harkens back to the heyday of the station wagon, which is a major memory of Boomer childhood).

From *Old Spice* to *Red Zone*

Here's another product that missed with Gen X. The case study is spelled out in a 2004 *BusinessWeek* magazine headline that reads:

"Extreme Makeover: How Procter & Gamble is selling once stodgy Old Spice to a whole new generation."

Old Spice deodorant: it's been around forever, it seems. In the mid-'90s, Procter rebranded it *Old Spice High Endurance,* but found that the twenty-five to forty-five age demo (at that time, older Gen X and younger Boomer guys) remembered Old Spice "as a relic from Dad's (or Granddad's) era." So P&G decided, in essence, to skip

Gen X and aim instead at very young Millennial boys by handing out samples of re-rebranded *Red Zone* to fifth-grade health classes, covering some 90 percent of the nation's schools and beginning in 1999. As P&G says in that *BusinessWeek* story, by 2001 Red Zone had become the top teen deodorant brand.

Street-smart
Cut the hype
The anti-commercial commercial

Xers take great pride in their street savvy. They've been marketed to all of their lives. They've seen every trick in the book. They can't be fooled. They don't want hype. *So don't even try.* This generation doesn't merely laugh at phony marketing messages. They aggressively *deride* them.

So some marketers have succeeded with Gen X with the anti-commercial commercial. No outlandish claims. You won't get the pretty girl or the handsome guy at the party if you buy our product. You won't score the winning goal in the big game. It's just a good product.

Nike's slogan – *Just Do It* – is quintessential Gen X messaging. *Let's cut the crap. If you want to look fit, if you want a vigorous energy and lifestyle, the reality is this: there are no lazy shortcuts. Just do it.*

Fabulous slogan. And an acknowledgement of – and a salute to - Xers' marketing savvy.

And in the 1990s, in an attempt to create brand loyalty with young Xers in the brutal soft drink wars, Sprite enjoys a very successful campaign with its anti-commercial commercials. One TV spot cuts back and forth – from a barber boasting to a customer, to a young adult playground braggart telling his buddy – that *they* taught basketball star Kobe Bryant all he knows about the game. After lots of braggadocio, the voiceover finally jumps in with this cut-the-crap outburst:

"Who ya gonna listen to? How 'bout yourself!!?" And then we read, onscreen, the text that carries the theme of this major advertising campaign: "Obey your thirst."

Xer Nation

As mentioned in our Boomer section, every generation steadily works its way to the top and then spends about fifteen to twenty years leading America's major institutions, applying its generation's own unique core values and beliefs to its leadership of those institutions.

Beginning in about 2012 or so, Gen X will begin *sharing* with Boomers the leadership positions at the very top of American government, business, education, religion, media, sport, and our nation's other influential institutions. There will be a temporary overlap of generational values at the top.

And by about 2020 or so, as Boomers retire (if they ever do; remember, this generation is empowered and engaged and wants to continue to contribute), we'll become a Gen X Nation for the next ten to fifteen years before Xers themselves share, and then ultimately hand off, those leadership reins to the Millennials, who will then take their Turn At The Top.

Their Future

Xers, here are four big questions your generation will soon answer:

When you lead America, will you be extremely ethical or extremely unethical? You came of age during an era that will be remembered as an extreme of unethical, greedy, and even criminal leadership of some of America's major institutions. Usually, American children growing up in one extreme either fully embrace that extreme or they recoil from it and defiantly do the exact opposite. They seldom settle in the middle.

So, when you take your turn at the top, will your generation be extremely unethical and selfish and greedy because you assume that's simply the way it's done in America? Or will you be extremely ethical and selfless? I routinely ask this question of Xer audience members at my presentations and consulting assignments around America, and consistently their thoughtful and sincere answer is, "I don't know how we'll be, as a generation."

What kind of American family unit will you create? You came of age when the American family was taking a pretty bad beating from divorce, mobile society, time poorness, and permissive parenting. So, what kind of family life will you create? Will you divorce in big numbers, as your parents did? Can you find the work-life balance your generation seeks so you can *be there for my kids*? Or, is American business facing such fierce competition with emerging and hungry workaholic nations that your generation won't be permitted to enjoy a "normal" workweek as it so passionately wishes to do?

What will your kids be like? Are you going to pass on to your children the same cynicism, disempowerment, and disengagement that you *understandably* developed during your own childhood, when the adult world was frequently letting you down and you felt powerless to correct it? Or instead, will you imbue your kids with optimism, hope, and empowerment by the things you say and do in their presence? We'll have to wait until your children pass through their formative years until we get a clear read of their generation's permanent core values and, thus, the answer to this question.

Will you ever "engage"? Will you *plug in* to the democratic process someday, as a generation? Will you vote in elections in bigger numbers than you now do? Will your generation's best members – or worst – pursue elected office and run our national, state, and local governments? Will you begin to read your daily newspaper and develop an appetite for factual and unbiased accounts of your world? Or will you stick with the personal-opinion blogs and the mocking TV shows? Will you ever feel empowered?

Your generation brings unique values, attitudes, skills, and priorities to American life. It seems your members *want* to contribute, *want* to plug in, *want* to make a positive difference, *want* to do the right thing. And our discouraged nation urgently needs for you to do so.

What will it take – from others, and from yourselves – to empower and engage you?

Chapter 9

Marketing To Xers
Tips, tactics, and guidelines

REMEMBER:

Generational messaging, executed properly, can deliver the one solution every marketer seeks. In an era when American consumers are bombarded by an estimated *3,500 to 5,000 messages per day* (as told to *USA Today* in 2005 by J. Walker Smith of research firm Yankelovich), generationally strategized messaging can *cut through the clutter.*

Xers are a numerically small generation. Only fifty-nine million born.

Many of their younger members still face sizable college and/or credit card debt, as well as uncertain job and income security. Can your marketing message empathize with them?

Xers experienced a materially comfortable but psychologically difficult childhood. "Uncertainty" is the operative word of their formative years. Leaders in government, business, religion, sport, and other major institutions were caught lying and cheating and failing. Commercial radio and television frequently seemed more interested in exploiting them – tricking them into listening or watching – instead of serving them. Big business was laying off their moms and dads. Divorce rates were skyrocketing. The family unit was weakening.

So this generation grew up skeptical and often cynical of older generations and institutions. They offer loyalty cautiously if at all, and most willingly to their fellow Xers, but frequently not to major institutions.

They also grew up spending less time in the presence of older people than prior generations had. There is a significant disconnect between many Xers and older people.

Gen X is a "me" generation: self-reliant, independent, individualistic, self-focused. Survival of the fittest. *What's in it for me?"*

The one industry that held such career promise for this generation – information technology – crashed in 2000, and now tech jobs are being sent to cheaper overseas labor. That, combined with significant debt (as one *Cincinnati Enquirer* newspaper headline pinpoints it, "We Are The Deep-In-Debt Generation") and the Xer inclination to change jobs frequently, is having a negative impact on their financial stability.

Because they experienced what sociologists label "premature wealth" as a result of their dual-career-income parents, a significant number of Xers were showered with expensive "things" during their formative years. Xers grew up with refined tastes. They know quality. And to the greatest extent that their incomes permit today, they demand and purchase quality.

As the first generation of youth to have "their own" radio stations and their own TV channels, Xers have been heavily marketed to, and advertised to, their entire lives.

From all of this come core values and attitudes and self-perceptions such as these:

- They take great pride in their individuality. They see themselves as millions of diverse individuals.
- They consider themselves a non-racist generation and take pride in their acceptance and tolerance of different ethnicities and lifestyles.
- They are very street smart and advertising savvy.
- They insist upon a work/personal life balance. They don't want to be workaholics like their parents.
- They need to be convinced. They grew up in a time of one broken promise after another.
- The people they feel they can trust tend to be people their own age. Think of the theme song of the TV show *Friends* when thinking of Xers: *"The job's a joke, you're broke... but I'll be there for you."*
- Xers have grown up to be pragmatic. As a generation, they espouse few, if any, sweeping ideologies or causes. They'll do what it takes to get through their own lives. They'll focus on a much smaller "world" that they feel they can influence.
- What matters most to them is their own immediate environment. National and international news and

events are often deemed irrelevant to their lives. *My life is all about my neighborhood, my kids' school district, my job. Things I can actually see, touch, and have some control over. And see the results of my work.*

- Many of them don't "feel" like a generation as strongly as other generations do. Their formative years delivered almost no positive historic events that gave this generation a sense of a "shared center." But they ARE a generation, very clearly defined.

- With a lack of positive historic events to cling to, pop culture from their formative years assumes large proportion in their lives. They like to poke fun at it, but *it's what they have,* so it's also uncommonly important to them. Celebrities, music, fashion, TV, movies.

- They grew up with a sense of disempowerment, a feeling that they cannot effect change in major institutions like government and big business. This has led to a disinterest in politics, voting, national causes, and hard news.

- Many of them do not know that the name *Generation X* is actually a badge of honor, not an insult.

TIPS, TACTICS, GUIDELINES – MARKETING TO XERS

Remember, Gen X passed through its formative years during the '70s, '80s, and '90s. In terms of pop culture, Xers shared the '70s with the Boomers, they shared the '90s with the first of the Millennials, but the 1980s are mostly Gen X. If you use "retro" messaging to reach Gen X, focus on these three decades.

Xers are easily bored. They enjoy unexpected and clever tricks and surprises in advertising.

Xers came of age with commercial radio and television force-feeding them a 24/7 message that fame and celebrity and wealth are *everything*. Although wised up, Xers remain more tuned in to the latest celebrity news than older generations. When you think Xers, think *People* magazine. It's slightly different for Millennials. Instead of just *following* celebrity comings and goings, Millennials – with all of the Internet's social networks making their own faces and stories reachable by the entire world – want to become famous celebrities *themselves*.

In commercial media, cruelty works with Xers. From its inception, television has always produced shows featuring talent competition and athletic competition. And always before, shows like Ted Mack's *Original Amateur Hour*, Ed McMahon's *Star Search*, and the others treated all contestants with respect and compassion, *especially* the ones who lost. But Xer viewers drove *Survivor* and *American Idol* into the TV ratings stratosphere. The one difference between these Xer-targeted concepts and prior shows of this genre? The element of "real" cruelty. *Survivor* closed each show with one competitor being cruelly berated and tossed off the show by the others. *American Idol's* big hook? Cruelty, again. Especially, the verbal bludgeoning of contestants by talent judge Simon Cowell that sometimes reduces contestants to tears. And don't forget Donald Trump's TV show, *You're Fired!* The TV ratings don't lie. As a programming strategy, "real" cruelty works with Xers. During the question-answer session that followed my Generational Marketing Strategy workshop with radio and TV folks from the South Carolina

Broadcasters Association in Columbia, one Boomer TV exec asked, "Why? Why do Xers respond to this kind of real cruelty on TV?" I turned to Xers in the audience for an answer. One Xer female said, "Because it makes us feel better about our own lives."

Treat Xers as individuals. They don't feel like a generation, even though they most definitely are. Don't let them think you view them as one big homogeneous target market. Xers don't like the *idea* of somebody being able to slot and pigeonhole them as a single "demo." In truth, you can slot them because they do share a massive common core.

Give them options. Xers demand "choices." One size does not fit all with this age cohort.

They have few trustworthy "heroes" from their formative years. Instead, the mass media flooded them with "celebrities" or "superstars" with clay feet, who regularly let them down. So choose celebrity product endorsers *very* carefully.

Humor. Xers' sense of humor has been described as one of "ironic detachment." Thus far in life, they feel they've wielded little power and have to take what they can get. So Xers like cynicism and skepticism in the messages that target them. But there might be a change coming, as Xers now gain more empowerment in their careers and family lives. Be alert for a possible pivot in the direction of positivism.

Trust. Generally speaking, they don't trust the media. Don't trust government. Don't trust big business. *If it's big, I probably can't trust it. It has never done anything to help me.* They do not accept media information – including the news – at face value.

Brand. Xers came of age with advertising that promoted brand more than features. Think Nike. Brand is important to Xers. For example, some hotel chains now pursuing Xers are making it a point to furnish their rooms with high-profile, Xer-friendly brands: everything from the TV set to the radio to the bathroom faucet to the booze in the honor bar. When older generations were coming of age, advertising was more features oriented than brand oriented.

Video games. Xer boys were the first big gamers and still make heavy use of them in adulthood. Female Xers are gaming in increasing numbers.

Don't be linear with your message. Add some twists and turns, irony and mystery. Some layers.

They value their Gen X peers, their friendships. Again, think along the lines of the TV sitcom *Friends.* If you want to sell your product to Phoebe, you must sell it to Rachel and Monica too. Xers trust Xers.

Celebrate the pride Xers take in their diversity and eclecticism and tolerance of alternative ideas.

Celebrate their self-reliance and independence.

To split hairs, Xers like the term "retro" more than "nostalgia." Nostalgia suggests "sentimentality," and they're not an especially sentimental generation. Emotional pitches and sentimental pitches will probably work better with all of the *other* generations. Berry Burst Cheerios used the retro 1970s pop tunes *I Think I Love You* by the Partridge Family and the 1974 B.J. Thomas song, *Hooked on a Feeling*. The campaign was "a huge success," according to the marketing manager for the brand.

Give them respect.

Anti-commercial commercials have worked well with this generation. These efforts at no-nonsense honesty convey respect for Xers' street savvy.

Attitude. Attitude. Attitude. Deliver attitude. Xers possess attitude and rejoice in it.

Have some fun. And make your fun off center, a little cockeyed. Most of the dot-com ads of the 1990s delivered this droll, way-off-center creative approach to advertising. But a caution: despite the clever creative of their advertising, many of those dot-com businesses also failed.

Emphasize pragmatism. This is not a visionary change-the-world generation. Life is about survival and doing the best you can. Life is about making sound, ordinary decisions, one at a time.

Xers do not prefer a lot of text. Instead, they prefer colorful, moving images. Silents and Boomers are the ones who prefer text.

According to a 2006 study of direct mail by research firm Vertis, 85 percent of women 25 – 44 (essentially, Xers) read printed direct mail marketing pieces. 53 percent of them read email advertisements. Discounts and special offers seem to enhance reader response to direct mail.

Make it participatory. Xers like interactivity. They're not passive users of media. They want to sample media and make their own choices and judgments.

Xers usually need more assurance than other generations. So, position your message to send positive and reinforcing signals. Reduce their risk.

Generation X: think "diversity." Ethnic diversity and lifestyle diversity.

The GAP and Old Navy are among marketers that have done well with multigenerational marketing and advertising strategies. Gen X seems to like this style. For example, Boomer-era pop music from the early 1970s, but with on-camera talent from Gen X.

One of the more high-visibility, multigenerational (Boomer + Gen X) campaigns occurred during Super Bowl 2003: the various Pepsi Twist spots that aired during the game. One spot magically morphed straitlaced and squeaky-clean Donny and Marie Osmond into the wacky Ozzy Osbourne family. *The Cincinnati Enquirer* asked a panel of mostly Gen Xers to judge the Super Bowl commercials that year, and Pepsi Twist was easily the most highly rated, with panelist comments such as "It integrated every generation," "It was cross-generational," and "It had all the different American icons (from different generations)."

Xers consider much of the pop culture of their youth to be cheesy, tacky, and begging for sarcasm, *but it's ours and we love to talk about it.* VH1's television series *I Love*

The '80s (also, *I Love The '70s*; also, *I Love The '90s*) is one such success story of reaching Xers by having moderately known comic wise guys and wise girls view a TV or movie clip or fashion photo or celebrity from those years and then ridicule it.

E-commerce:

- Speed is essential. Fast results. So, make your e-commerce swift but exciting, with a sense of discovery.
- Make your Web site address fun and memorable.
- With download speed in mind, keep your Web site's heavy graphics and video on inside pages, not your home page.
- Keep your pages short and visually stimulating.
- Give this skeptical generation of consumers your after-sale assurance by making your contact information easy to see and complete in its instructions. Many e-commerce sites are absolutely miserable at this, especially in the technology sector.
- Give them a feedback link. Xers visit your site for information, but they also want to interact with it.

Parenthood:

- Many Xers grew up in nontraditional households. They want their own children to have a sense of family and roots and tradition, but they might not be sure how to create it, because they didn't have it as kids themselves. *Help them.* Mommy Web sites and blogs, for example.
- The ultimate Gen X TV show is *Friends*. And one of that show's primary messages is this, according to *TIME* magazine (April 19, 2004): "There is no *normal*

anymore.... The characters have dealt with one problem: how to replace the kind of family in which they grew up with the one they believed they were supposed to have." If you can market a product or service that helps Xers to figure this out, you win.

- Gen X moms have replaced Boomer moms as the dominant purchasers of children's toys. And Xers want toys that are fun *and* educational. They want their kids to play and learn at the same time. Fisher-Price, in 2004, based its biggest television-advertising push ever on this generational core value.
- Xer dads want to be involved in their kids' lives. Research documents that fathers who volunteer at school can have a profound effect on their children's academic success. So find a way to catch this Dad Wave.
- Xer parents feel they don't have as much time to spend with their children as they would like. And they know how beneficial it would be to the kids if they did spend more time with them. The primary obstacle is the parents' work schedules. If your products and services can somehow genuinely help to overcome this angst, you can score big with this generation.

Home decorating. Xers are more likely than older generations to *mix* décor styles. According to New York research company PortiCo Research, Xers focus on decorating one room at a time so it meets their exact specifications. Xer men are more involved in decorating decisions than older generations of men. Embrace both the woman and man.

Xers will have done their homework when they enter the store but will still need help. Customer service might become the make-or-break for the retailer.

Xers love stories. Don't give them just bullet points in your marketing and advertising. Tell stories.

Find the good. From 1983's *A Nation at Risk* report and thereafter, the people of Generation X have grown up hearing and seeing their generation labeled as underachievers, slackers. Marketers and advertisers face a significant opportunity: celebrate the good in this generation, its positive values and skills and qualities, tell Xers about their generation in ways they've never heard so they will celebrate themselves.

Female denigration backlash. Marketers, in their attempt to reach Xer men, have spent a long time pedaling what the masses call "sleaze," especially in ways that denigrate Gen X women. Make no mistake, there must be something to this strategy, because some of those marketers have made a lot of money from Xer men. But in early 2004, a public backlash against the beer commercials began, and now today the beers have pretty much pulled away from the female denigration. Consider carefully before you decide whether to use the denigration of women in order to get the attention of Xer men. This strategy is currently in limbo.

Gen X and the Web: Internet use by any generation is still in constant flux. If I listed the top ten sites for Gen X men and Gen X women, the list might be obsolete by the time you finished reading this sentence. So you'll have to do your own research on this. But generally speaking, Xer men's more popular sites have been much more *varied* than those of Xer women, whose top sites thus far have been dominated by *retail* sites for fragrances and cosmetics, jewelry and luxury goods, toys, apparel, and so on. The men, conversely, bounce from gaming to automotive to sports to travel to entertainment to porn, and others.

Chapter 10

Xers In The Workplace
Tips, tactics, and guidelines

Now to Gen X at work:

- They will be the generation that eventually replaces the Boomers at the top.*
- They're creative, entrepreneurial.
- Self-reliant and independent.**
- Technologically savvy.

* Is your organization systematically evaluating Gen X's aptitude for leadership, training them to replace Boomers and become leaders (which will not come as effortlessly to Xers as it has to Boomers), ensuring a stress-reduced mcthod to transfer the Boomers' intellectual capital and practical intelligence to them?

** "Self-reliant and independent." Sound ordinary? Take it for granted? Wait 'til we get to the Millennials.

- Individualistic, results oriented.
- Self-focused rather than team.*
- Don't expect or promise loyalty.
- Career free agents.
- Probably won't give us a bumper crop of leaders.**

* Don't underestimate the "I'm-in-it-for-me" attitude of this generation. The adult world they witnessed during their formative years has engendered a self-protective attitude. Xers and Millennials are job-hopping, "churning," much more than Boomers, Silents, and G.I.s did at that age.

** (This is a copy-and-paste insert from the Boomer section). If you compile a list of attributes that are essential to great leadership, you'll probably place a check mark beside every one of them when evaluating the Boomer Generation. Hard workers. Willing to go the extra mile. Team players. Excellent interpersonal skills. Loyal to, and concerned about the entire organization and all employees, not just themselves. Bold, visionary, assertive. Willing to take risks. Willing to risk failure. Willing to be accountable for their actions. Etc., etc. It's simple to explain: beyond their own control, the formative years of Boomers – the times and teachings they absorbed back then – just happened to mold core values perfectly suited for leadership, just as the formative years of G.I.s and now the Millennials have done. Silents have not given us a bumper crop of leaders, and it's likely Xers won't either because their formative years did *not* mold that same long list of leadership traits *and that's okay.* Silents and Xers are especially skilled at *executing* and *implementing* the visions of their just-older generations. After hearing this in my recent Washington, D.C. seminar for representatives of the Veterans Administration Medical Centers, a Gen X surgeon came up and said what other Xer audience members around the country have echoed: "I don't think our generation especially *wants* to lead," she said. "I think our values line up perfectly for execution and implementation. Leadership doesn't hold a lot of prestige for us, because leaders were pretty rotten when we were growing up."

- Comfortable with change.
- Global perspective.
- Willing to work hard.
- Want to make money and succeed.*
- Seek work/play balance.

* It's just that, sometimes, Xers want to do things differently from the ways they've been done before. And all they request, boss, is that you'll be open to their suggestions and give them a chance.

- At ease with ethnic, lifestyle diversity.
- Open-minded.
- They're career gender benders.*

* Colleges and trade schools report an increase in males pursuing careers in traditionally female professions. And women are entering professions once held mainly by men.

- Might be skeptical of elders, big corporations.
- Every job is temporary.
- Every company is a steppingstone.*

- Not as aggressive as Boomers.**

* Xers are not genetically programmed to job-hop. They would love to enjoy stimulation, fulfillment, and advancement with one employer, but they came of age seeing too many bosses dismantle the traditional two-way loyalty with employees, so this "steppingstone" attitude is an acknowledgement that Xers can't count on loyalty from, and longevity with, one employer, so they'd better be always ready to move on and seek other opportunities.

** Boomers, a massive generation, had to grow up competitive with each other, aggressive. So they're comfortable with others who are the same way. Boomers *expect* others to push back hard when they disagree with them. The much smaller Gen X will never face the same kind of competition and so tends to be a little less competitive and aggressive in the workplace. Many of my human resource clients repeat the same frustration: "If a Boomer employee is dissatisfied for some reason, she'll come right to the boss and fight for what she wants. But when Xers become dissatisfied on the job, we don't hear about it until, one day out of nowhere, they give us their two-week notice!" As a generation, Xers often don't demonstrate the same kind of aggressiveness as Boomers. This has become a significant generation gap in the workplace. Boomers: be careful that your natural assertiveness doesn't overwhelm, dominate, and suffocate those Xers who won't fight back as vigorously as you fully expect – and *want* – them to do. Don't fall into the easy trap of dominating the dialogue around the conference table. Xers: it's okay to make your point assertively; to Boomers, that's normal. Fight fair, but fight hard for what you believe.

- Work to live, not live to work.
- Many prefer start-ups, small firms.
- Might choose a city first, and then find a job.*
- Might not socialize with coworkers.

* Many Xers seek a certain way of life that some cities and towns offer and others don't. So they move to a favored city and then try to establish their career. Cities like Seattle, Minneapolis, Columbus, Cleveland, Denver, and others have worked hard to become destinations for Gen X professionals. This is why my list of consulting clients includes local and state economic development departments that want to proactively create recruitment initiatives that will lure and retain these professionals. Some cities are connecting with Gen X, some aren't.

- Don't buy "pay-your-dues" approach (it requires two-way loyalty, which Xers don't trust).
- Demanding attitude: want it fast.
- Seek skill-building opportunities.
- Seek respect and input.

Recruiting Xers

- Explain time demand up front.*
- Can you explain career path?
- Enhance their skill set.
- Be technologically forward.
- Reward individualism, creativity.

* If, in an average year, there will be peaks and valleys in the hours required, outline those peaks and valleys

with Xer job candidates during the recruitment period – right away! In as much detail as possible! **This is the single-biggest complaint I hear from my clients in all of my generational consulting.** Nationwide and across many industries, the complaint is always the same. Managers explain, "Our business is not always a perfect 9-to-6 world. Sometimes, we face a crunch and we need our people to put in extra hours, and the other generations understand and accept this, but our Xers draw a hard line on start-and-stop time, and when the clock strikes normal-quitting-time, they're gone."

One General Sales Manager at a major-market TV station said, "There are certain times of the year when the advertising sales team at a television station has only a couple of weeks to sell advertising for a major upcoming TV season or single event. It's now or never. Consistently during those crunch weeks, my Boomer salespeople are still at their cubicles at 8 or 10 p.m.; they understand. But all of my Xers left at 6."

And in Texas, after I had presented a training session to the Texas Society of Certified Public Accountants, a principal in one firm shared this story. "We recently had a Gen X female accountant *time her pregnancy so she would be on maternity leave during tax season, which is our crunch time!*"

And a physician's group affiliated with a hospital in South Carolina shared a similar story. A female physician was consistently refusing to respond to off-hours calls from patients, and her mostly Boomer colleagues were having to cover for her.

But here's a more positive anecdote. It comes from another client of mine, one of the country's larger commercial construction companies, based in Atlanta. An Xer employee and I were discussing this same workplace dilemma after my presentation to that company's management team, and here's what he said: "I quit my previous job with another construction company because, in the summer months, the work mushroomed up to seventy hours a week, and I want to see my son's baseball games. So, I started looking around and interviewed with *this* company. I told them about my commitment to my kids and they did their best to explain, up front, when the peaks and valleys would occur, and we're trying to find the middle ground. I know I can't have it perfectly because I've chosen construction for my career and that means lots of work in the warm-weather months. But the company is demonstrating good faith and I figure they're doing the best they can to help me with my work-life balance. The key is, we talked about this potential conflict and got it on the table at the right time: during the recruitment process."

Managing Xers

- Remember: to Xers, career success – work-life balance.
- Offer mentoring.
- Don't micromanage.
- Establish a refined and continuous retention program to deal with the churn of Xer employees.
- Train them constantly. With Xers, this can build loyalty.
- If an Xer leaves, remember that you might get him or her back, down the road; make the Xer's departure cordial and maintain contact.

- Quantify performance – don't just pat 'em on the back; measure their performance and put it in writing.
- Give them plenty of resources.
- Give them constant feedback.*
- Permit them input and feedback.**

* Some companies practice the 360-degree performance review, in which employers and employees review each other anonymously. And Xers appreciate the sense of input and involvement that this policy permits.

** If your management team is Boomer and/or Silent, open up the communications lines with Xers: ask-me-anything lunches, "fireside chats," and regular meetings, all designed to shrink the generation gaps and give Xers authentic input, an authentic stake in the organization.

- Be alert for ethics.*
- Be alert for self-focus.*
- Be alert for cynicism, pessimism, distrust.*

* Beyond their control, Xers came of age during a time of widespread corruption and unethical behavior in so many corners of American society. They might assume this is the norm. They might also possess a strong self-focus that doesn't fit with your organization's team focus. Ditto with possible cynicism, pessimism, and distrust.

I've phrased these caveats with the words "be alert for" because you shouldn't assume them. A big percentage of Xers share the same ethics, sense of team, and optimism with older generations. But because of their generation's experience of youth, these caveats are "possibles" you'll simply want to be on the lookout for. And Xers will welcome your guidance and help in doing what's right.

- Number of single dads growing.*
- Returning moms.**
- Flexible schedules for Mom and Dad: extended maternity leave and pay? Transfers to positions with less travel?***
- Can you help them with their time-poorness and create programs to enhance their work-life balance?****

* According to the Census Bureau, in 1970 there were only 393 thousand single-father families in America. In the 2000 census, there were more than 2 million, a fivefold increase in thirty years. Be sensitive to single dads; they are more likely than single moms to fear career consequences for using company benefits related to childrearing. What's more, because of the newness of *dads* having child custody, they don't have the social support system from other single dads that single moms have been able to develop over a longer period of time.

** Mothers today are reversing a thirty-year trend and are choosing to stay at home in increasing numbers. And research shows this is going to continue. But these Gen X – and Boomer – mothers who left their jobs to raise children and then tried to come back are frequently having a tough time because of that hole in their resumés. And so some companies are trying to accommodate motherhood. Deloitte & Touche developed what it calls a "Personal Pursuits" program that will permit employees to take various kinds of unpaid leave – including maternity leave – for several years. The company will offer periodic training sessions and will assign mentors to keep them current so they can return and hit the ground running. It hopes to cut down on turnover costs by rehiring these people after their leaves expire.

*** A *Wall Street Journal* story described Accenture's "Future Leave" program, whereby the company helps employees to set aside, in advance, part of their pay to finance up to three *extra* months of leave, with benefits. But there's also somewhat of a backlash to generous maternity leave. A 2007 survey – with a ± 4 percent margin of error – by the world's largest employment agency Adecco, shows that 20 percent of surveyed women and 25 percent of surveyed men agree with the statement, "I am often left picking up the slack for my coworkers who are moms." Asked if they perceive coworker resentment about flexible hours for mothers, 59 percent of men aged thirty-five to forty-four said "yes."

To be fair to employees on maternity leave, can you prorate annual performance quotas to adjust for time on leave?

**** Progressive Insurance provides on-site healthcare counseling and errand-running services such as photo developing and dry-cleaning. So think outside the box. Take-home dinners? On-site day care, and perhaps elder care?

- Make training visual and brief.
- Teach application over theory.
- Teach hard and soft skills.
- Teach accountability.*

- Teach business courtesy.*
- Teach interpersonal skills.*
- Train Xers – especially management and leadership candidates – in Generational Workforce Diversity.**

* Because of the unique times during their formative years, Xers might need training or mentoring in soft skills such as accepting responsibility and being accountable for their actions, common courtesy, and interpersonal skills. After a seminar in Generational Human Resource Strategy at a big-city hospital, a male Gen X employee said, "I have two close friends, and we've talked about this. We were lucky; our parents drilled courtesy into us as we grew up. And when competing with other Xers for jobs or promotions, we actually use our courtesy as a competitive weapon against our fellow Xers."

** Gen X, because its members came of age spending less time in the presence of older people than other generations had done, will benefit from this training. And the other generations will benefit by learning about the one generation they understand least: Xers.

- Judge Xers by merit, not seniority.
- Create a fun atmosphere.
- Don't micromanage them.*
- Let them discover solutions their way.**

* Here's the message most Xers would like their bosses to embrace: "Boss, tell me where Point A is, where our organization is right now. Then tell me where Point Z is, where you want us to go. Give me the tools, give me the technology, and I'll get us there! And you know what?

If you give me respect and responsibility and the credit when it's over, I'll work past 6 p.m. to get it done!!"

** Xers are magnificent problem solvers and solution finders. This emanates from a long list of their unique core values, but especially from their independence and self-reliance. After I had presented a keynote speech about GenX to the national conference of the Community Leadership Association, the Executive Director of the Toledo chapter, a Boomer, walked up to the podium, carrying a hard copy of his chapter's Annual Report and beaming with pride. "I did just what you mentioned in your speech today," he said. "It wasn't easy because I'm a perfectionist. But when it was time to create the Annual Report, I gave the project to a staff of GenX writers, editors, and designers. I spelled out the broad parameters, but then decided – and this isn't always easy to do - to back off and let them run with this project on their own, and look at this! It's spectacular, and I wouldn't have done it as good myself!"

There is a magnificent marriage waiting to happen in the American workplace.

Boomers: you're brilliant at leadership and the big idea, but you need help in the _execution_.

Xers: your generation's brilliance is where the rubber meets the road, in finding the best method to _execute_ the big idea.

If you Boomers and Xers can understand your generational differences and identify your respective strengths and shortcomings, then perhaps you can grasp the enormity of the magic you can create *together*.

And if you ever make that connection, American industry will once again blow past the other nations of the world in innovation and output.

A magnificent marriage, waiting to happen....

Chapter 11

The Millennials
*The most adult-supervised kids
in American history*

FORMATIVE YEARS, CORE VALUES,
ADULTHOOD, FUTURE

**Born: 1982 – present (2007)
80 million and counting
Formative years: 1980s to ???**

The Millennial Generation. A dramatic departure from
the core values and attitudes of Gen X, because Millennials
are experiencing dramatically different formative years.

Where Gen X children had been the least adult-supervised generation, Millennials are the *most* adult-supervised. And their core values, as a result, are notably different from those of Xers.

They're more than eighty million strong, and we don't yet know in what year the Millennials will end and the next generation will begin. The Millennials will end for the same reasons that all American generations have ended and the next has begun: *because there is a substantial change in the times and/or the teachings that young children are going to absorb in their formative years that will create in them substantially different core values from the just-older generation.*

A couple of consultants had proclaimed "the end of the Millennials" a year or two after the terror attacks of September 11, 2001. They argued that the five-year-olds, or nine-year-olds, or seven-year-olds of that day do not have a clear memory of 9/11, and therefore their values will be different from those of the older kids, and therefore the Millennial Generation ends.

Oops.

In 2005, four years after 9/11, America experiences *Hurricane Katrina.* And wadda ya know? The *same list* of powerful generational core values burned into older Millennials from 9/11 – uncertainty about one's own physical safety; a strong sense of nation and patriotism; selflessness and helping total strangers in need – is now burned into *younger* kids who have no clear memory of 9/11 but formed the same values because of a similar and unpredictable moment in history. Especially because Katrina became a prominent discussion topic in America's classrooms.

And this experience with Katrina means the Millennial Generation is going to extend into younger-than-expected age brackets. As of 2007, we must live with the uncertainty, for an indeterminate period, of not knowing at what age the Millennials will end and America's next generation will begin. *We can't predict the future.*

Millennials' formative years began in the 1980s.

The most important message about marketing and advertising to Millennials is this:

Generational strategy is not reliable until kids reach *about* age seventeen, when they graduate from high school. I alert clients to this, and I've turned down other prospective clients who market a product or service to the age twelve-to-seventeen demo, or kids six to eleven. I tell them point-blank: generational values don't become crystallized and reliable until the late teens. Until that age, we're all just wacky, flighty "kids." On one day, young teens might announce, "We believe in sexual abstinence!!" But if, at tonight's concert, the lead singer of the band shouts out "Sex all the time!" those kids will say, "Yeah, sex all the time!"

Millennials' older members are now just beyond their formative years, and so we do identify some core values that will be reliable. So this book focuses upon *First-Wave* Millennials only, those born from 1982 to 1990.

We'll get to the Second-Wave "Mils" in a few years.

Bill Strauss and Neil Howe, in their 2000 book entitled *Millennials Rising,* wrote that these older Millennials were growing up to be very much like the G.I. Generation. And now, more than a half dozen years since that book was published, we also detect a lot of Baby Boomer in them, which is to be expected. We all are the products of our parents, and First-Wave Millennials have mostly Boomers (and some of the very oldest Xers) as parents.

Optimistic and enthusiastic
Pessimistic about their country's direction
Respectful of authority
Focused on their education
Close with their parents
Compassionate

Millennials are:

- optimistic and enthusiastic about their own future;
- pessimistic about their country's direction, especially in the late 2000s as Americans differ sharply on their government's handling of the multifront war against terrorism;
- respectful of authority – they're eager to change some things, but they'll work within the system;
- intensely focused on their education;
- enjoying very close and loving relationships with their parents;
- and, growing up to be compassionate towards others and outwardly rather than inwardly focused.

The television show *60 Minutes* recently aired a segment on the Millennials, who talked about their fast-paced lives, their pressures, their tech-dominated lives, their spending power. And then the reporter (Steve Kroft, I believe) asked a group of Millennial kids to talk about their parents. And these kids *gushed* with praise and gratitude. And from one research study to the next, their comments are consistent:

They're fantastic. I love my parents. My best friends. My teachers. Always there for me. And on and on.

Coca-Cola promptly jumped on this strong sense of gratitude that Millennials feel toward their nurturing and protective parents with a humorous and memorable TV spot.

In this thirty-second spot, we see a Millennial teenage boy open the refrigerator door and start searching. He sees just *one* Coca-Cola. He reaches for it just as his Boomer Dad, off-camera in another room of the house, shouts out "Chris, is there any more Coke?" As Chris decides whether to keep the Coke for himself by lying, or give the last one to Dad, the spot cuts to three flashbacks as Chris recalls some recent events between Dad and himself:

1. Dad is teaching him how to drive; and as they sit in the car in the driveway, with Dad instructing him to put the car in "drive" and go forward, the son mistakenly shifts into "reverse" and backs the car right through the garage door, but Dad simply gives him an encouraging pat on the shoulder.
2. Next, Dad is sitting at the kitchen table doing some paperwork as the son, practicing golf in the backyard, drives a ball right through the window, showering dad with broken glass, but Dad reacts calmly.
3. Finally, Dad opens the bathroom door just in time to see his son shaving half of his scalp in order "to get the right look for graduation"; Dad quietly closes the door and respectfully leaves his son to all of his teenage goofiness.

The spot ends by returning to a shot of Chris at the refrigerator, making his decision to give Dad the last Coke, "Yeah, got one right here," with the word "gratitude" typed on the screen.

Excellent messaging to the Millennials' core value of gratitude toward their parents.

Declining sales of rap and hip-hop

The Millennial Generation's optimism and closeness with their parents might also explain a March 2007 Associated Press story that states, "… after 30 years of popularity, rap music is now struggling with an alarming sales decline and growing criticism from within about the culture's negative effect on society."

According to this AP account, from 2005 to 2006 rap sales decreased a whopping 21 percent. And mathematically speaking, if rap simply had *held steady* with Millennials, sales should have *grown* because for every six Xers there are eight Millennials.

Rap's authentic rage and cynicism fit perfectly with the emotions of Gen X kids in the troubled '80s and '90s. But it apparently doesn't translate well with the soaring positivism of Millennials in the 2000s. And even Xers themselves, now in adulthood, are advancing their careers and families, chalking up some victories in life, and gaining a sense of empowerment that suggests the negativism of rap is connecting less and less with America's younger generations.

Rap insider Chuck Creekmur told Associated Press reporter Nekesa Mumbi Moody, "A lot of people are sick of rap... the negativity is just over the top now." And a study by the Black Youth Project showed a majority of black youth feel rap has too many violent images.

The American marketplace must understand shifts in generational core values.

Grade pressure
Time pressure
Adult-supervised

Millennials feel intense pressure to get good grades. They're a massive generation, like the Boomers, so the competition is ferocious to get admitted into their colleges of choice and to get the best possible entry-level jobs.

A new phenomenon is occurring among this generation's top academic performers: the triple major, the quadruple, and in some cases the quintuple major, just to try to get an advantage in landing the best entry-level job in an increasingly tight job market.

Millennials also feel time pressure and tend to schedule their days like efficiency experts.

When I hosted that earlier-mentioned generational talk show special for public TV stations, one of our featured guests was Myrtis Powell, vice president of Student Affairs at Miami University. When asked about the Millennials, she didn't hesitate. "These kids schedule everything. If they have a one-hour square on their electronic calendars that doesn't have some activity filled in, they panic!"

And importantly, much of their day is spent in adult-supervised activities, so in vivid contrast to Gen X, parents and other adults are a constant presence in the formative years of the Millennial Generation, and Millennials thus feel especially at ease around older people.

Team players
Community-active
Declining social pathology

They're team players.

Gen X came of age during times that molded them as a "Me" generation: individualistic and self-reliant.

Millennials, conversely, are a "We" generation.

Where Xers had come of age with the media isolation mentioned earlier, today's media constantly connect Millennials to other *human beings*, with cell phones, pagers, instant messaging, e-mail, social networks like MySpace, YouTube, FaceBook, and the others.

What's more, classes are often structured for group projects, in which all members of the group receive the same grade based upon the team performance.

There is recent media industry research indicating that Millennials often prefer to watch Hollywood movies at home on DVD with groups of friends, rather than going to a local movie theater. They can pause the movie at any time to talk about the movie and thus make it more of an interactive and group experience than when sitting in rows at the theater. A more "we-friendly" environment at home. Especially when you're so comfortable in the presence of Mom and Dad, and your friends' moms and dads, that you don't feel the need to flee the house.

September 11 and Katrina

The two historical events that will always define this generation and give its members a *shared center* are the terrorist attacks of 9/11 and the devastation of New Orleans and other parts of the Gulf Coast by Hurricane Katrina. Some Millennials call themselves the September Eleventh Generation.

Virginia Tech
04.16.07

The massacre of thirty-two students by a fellow student at Virginia Tech on April 16, 2007, is also likely to reinforce both the Millennials' uncertainty about their physical safety and their already-strong sense of "being a generation." Within hours of the shootings, other colleges around the country used e-mail and social networks to send messages of sympathy and support to the Virginia Tech students, giving all of them a sense of generational "us."

Generation Give

As a result of 9/11, and because most schools now make it a priority, Millennials are learning about, and embracing, the value of community service.

They've been labeled "Generation Give."

For many, it began with blood donations and school fundraisers in the 9/11 aftermath. Remember, the classroom is the great compressor, the great incubator, of generation-wide values. And Millennials were the ones discussing 9/11 and Katrina with their teachers in the classrooms, and their classmates in the cafeteria, after each disaster. These are value-forming historical events for this generation, just as the Great Depression, World War II, Cold War, Kennedy assassination, Watergate scandal, space shuttle Challenger explosion, and similar events had been for America's other generations.

A *USA Today* newspaper story headlined "Kids trade spring break for a chance to help" chronicles the new wave of "alternative spring breaks" amongst Millennial collegians, a wave coordinated by Campus Compact, a coalition of a thousand colleges committed to community service. Instead of heading for the traditional spring break of beaches/beers/babes/boys, students – in big numbers – are using spring break to help others. An estimated "tens of thousands" of college students reportedly poured into the Gulf states during spring break 2006 to help Katrina victims, even volunteering for the nastier cleanup work. Eighty-eight-year-old Rosemary Doran, whose house sat in eight feet of water, was helped by a group of Kansas collegians and said afterward, "I wish I could adopt them, they're so adorable."

Scott Harding, founder of the National Relief Network begun in the '90s to coordinate relief programs, told *USA Today* he's *never seen so many students who want to help.*

In 2006, applications to Teach For America, which recruits college grads to teach in underserved urban and rural areas, was triple the number of 2000 when the youngest Xers were graduating.

The Peace Corps took in the largest number of volunteers in thirty years, up more than 20 percent from 2000. And VISTA (Volunteers In Service To America) has enjoyed a similar surge in volunteers since Millennials began moving into adulthood.

And this Generation-Give core value is further reinforced in Millennials' minds because schools are stressing community service more than ever before, and community service looks good on a college or job application form, and this is a massive generation competing fiercely with each other in the workplace.

High School Community Service
1984: 900,000 U.S. students
2003: 6,200,000 U.S. students

Here's a comparison, and this is not a knock against Gen X; it's simply a reflection of changes in the times:

In 1984, as the first Xers were graduating from high school, 900,000 American high school students participated in volunteer community work as part of their school activities. In 2003, as the first Millennials were graduating, the number was seven times higher: 6,200,000 high school students.

Another "phenomenon" of sorts is also occurring during Millennials' formative years and is reinforcing even more this generational value of philanthropy.

When Gen X was coming of age, America was much more materialistic, and MTV and other teen-targeted media were hosing down Xer children with constant stories and images of *conspicuous consumption and self-indulgence by the rich and powerful*: actors, singers, business executives, and other super-rich spending lavishly on *themselves*. Mansions, fur coats, diamonds, weddings, travel, limousines, and on and on. Remember the TV show *Lifestyles of the Rich and Famous?*

But today, what are Millennials hearing and reading about the nation's wealthiest people during *their* generation's formative years? A slight change.

The Bill & Melinda Gates Foundation. Warren Buffett adding his own billions to the Gates Foundation mission. George Clooney, Oprah Winfrey, Brad Pitt and Angelina Jolie and other celebrities using their fame and wealth to help the less advantaged. Silicon Valley tech billionaires creating their own foundations.

We are the products of our formative years' times and teachings. And Millennials are forming generational values just as some high-profile Americans seem to be taking their wealth in a more selfless direction.

So these experiences are creating Millennial core values of patriotism, a sense of nation, empowerment and engagement, volunteerism, charity, and teamwork.

And those values will influence Millennial decision making for their entire lives.

Cause marketing to Millennials

Because of this, some prominent companies are directing "cause marketing" at Millennials. As a *BusinessWeek* magazine story about this strategy is headlined: "We're Good Guys, Buy from Us."

Target stores, American Outfitters, Timberland footwear, Nike, American Apparel, and others are in sync with research that says more than 60 percent of today's Millennials are more likely to buy brands that support charitable causes.

And, marketers know these young people also influence many major purchases by their moms and dads.

Declining social pathologies

And finally, many but not all teenage social pathologies are declining with Millennials: the teenage birth rate recently reached a sixty-year low with Millennials. Teen crime is down, as is teen smoking.

Drug and alcohol use by junior-high and high-school Millennials is generally down, according to a study by the

University of Michigan, although that age group's use of the painkiller Oxycontin reached a record high in 2006.

But with Millennials in college, recent research by The National Center on Addiction and Substance Abuse at Columbia University compares collegians' drug use in 1993 (when Xers filled our nation's campuses) and 2005, when Millennials dominated enrollments. And the study documents that the use of cocaine, marijuana, and illicit drugs in general is on the rise. Conversely, the use of hallucinogens and inhalants is declining.

Spirituality rising

Perhaps because of the terror attacks of September 11, Millennials are demonstrating a significant interest in their own spirituality, faith, and religion.

According to a *TIME* magazine report, when Millennials began reaching college age in the late '90s, enrollment at the nation's 104 "intentionally Christ-centered colleges" rose more than three times faster than enrollment at all four-year colleges. As one college senior told the magazine: *"Young people want to know something bigger than themselves."*

Problems and challenges

Make no mistake: this generation, like all others in their youth, faces major problems and challenges.

Binge drinking by eighteen- to twenty-year olds, and especially by high school and college *girls*, has escalated dramatically since the mid-'90s.

Commercial television, in its pursuit of Millennial spending dollars – and in this era of surging competition from New Media – has increased both the volume and the boldness of its sex content in its desperation to hold onto viewers.

So have books, music videos, music lyrics, Hollywood movies, magazines, the Internet, the apparel industry, professional sport, and virtually every other teen-targeted medium except one.

The one medium that has thus far refused to "race to the bottom," as this increased media vulgarity and sex bombardment of our nation's kids has been described, is the *daily newspaper.*

And, just like Gen Xers, Millennials are going through their formative years witnessing what they perceive to be the ethical and moral failure of some trusted adult institutions, because of:

- the Catholic priest sex abuse scandals;
- the epidemic of executive corruption atop corporate America;
- President Clinton and Monica Lewinsky;
- And, athletes on performance-enhancing drugs.

Helicopter parents

Here are several unanswered questions about this generation's upbringing that are attracting significant attention amongst us generational scholars, child psychologists, and sociologists.

Millennials are so heavily supervised by adults that child experts are now pretty certain they're over-parented: too dependent upon always-present and protective parents and other adults to develop the necessary independence and toughness they'll need as adults.

In fact, there's a label for these over-protective parents: "Helicopter Parents," because they're constantly hovering around their children, ready to swoop in and rescue them anytime there's a problem.

And the most extreme such parents have now been nicknamed after the most "extreme" model of our nation's military helicopters and are called "Blackhawk Parents."

Most people applaud this parental protectiveness; the only question is one of degree. Interviews with Millennials say they like the parental involvement.

But child psychologists – and even some parents themselves – fear over-parenting.

After my recent presentation on Generational Workforce Diversity and Human Resource Strategy to the Ontario Nurses Association conference in Toronto, one Boomer mother confessed, "I've been a helicopter parent of my nine-year-old son. I knew I was over-protecting him, knew he needed to learn and correct mistakes on his own, couldn't help myself, asked my husband to help me to give our boy some breathing room but that didn't work either, and I didn't know how to divert my constant attention from my son so I bought a puppy."

She added with a giggle, "I now have the most nurtured dog in Canada."

Campus counseling

On another matter:

According to a recent survey of college counseling center directors, there has been a dramatic escalation on the college campuses of Millennial students seeking psychological counseling, which experts feel is directly related to their over-structured, over-parented, hyperactive schedules. Here's the list: severe psychological problems, anxiety, panic attacks, substance abuse, eating disorders, self-inflicted injury, and even withdrawal from college. At some colleges, at the time of this study, the waiting list to schedule a second counseling appointment was four to six *weeks*.

Free play

This is a generation growing up with much less free play than prior generations enjoyed.

Psychiatrist Stuart Brown, in California, founded the Institute for Play because of his concern, and in a magazine interview, he told parents:

"When you rush around delivering them to all those structured activities, it tells them you want them to be hyperactive, over-achieving, over-scheduled workaholics, and that's what they could very well become as adults."

Rich-poor separation

Another concern: the rich-poor separation in this country is returning; white flight from integrated public schools is growing, and schools are re-segregating; the cost of teenage technology – cell phones, pagers, computers, Internet, cable TV – is creating a generation of Millennial "haves" and "have-nots."

How will this influence their generation's lifelong core values?

"Girls are on a tear."
"Boys are falling behind."

One final concern about Millennials, which continues a problem that began with Gen X: overlooking the boys.

Thirty years ago, in the early '70s, educational experts launched the Girl Project to wipe out girls' historical weaknesses in certain subjects. Schools focused on girl-sensitive education, and it worked then and continues to work today.

Here's a recent quote from Thomas Mortenson, a senior

scholar at the Pell Institute:

"Girls are on a tear through the educational system. In the past thirty years, nearly every inch of educational progress has gone to them."

And Harvard professor William Pollock adds:

"It's not just that boys are falling behind girls. It's that the boys are falling behind their own functioning and doing worse than they ever did before."

Families and little moments

Here's another concern about the formative years of both Xers and Millennials:

Since the 1970s, when the birth-control pill and the women's movement gave us dual-career, fast-paced, time-starved parents, two generations of children have missed out on, as one Associated Press story explains, the "little moments:"

the million-and-one tiny instances in a child's formative years when that child learns just another *inch* – another tiny morsel – of general information about life, just by spending lots of *relaxed* and *unhurried* hours in the physical presence of Mom and Dad, listening to them, talking with them, *absorbing.*

In their childhoods, many Millennials and Xers were not exposed to those million-and-one morsels that most Boomer, Silent, and G.I. kids absorbed just because they spent so many more hours in the physical presence of their parents over the first seventeen or eighteen years of their lives. And those morsels and little moments accumulate into a body of knowledge and understanding that is very substantial.

The UCLA Center on Everyday Lives of Families

The Alfred P. Sloan Foundation is sponsoring a sizable study by UCLA of the intersection between American family life and work. Although just underway, trends are emerging related to the biggest change in family dynamics in forty years: mothers working outside the home. From an Associated Press story about this study:

"Parents and children live virtually apart at least five days a week, reuniting for a few hours at night."

Study director Elinor Ochs concludes, 'We've outsourced a lot of our relationships... there isn't much room for the flow of life, those little moments when things happen spontaneously.'"

And Ochs is especially concerned about this: "Returning home at the end of the day is one of the most delicate and vulnerable moments in life. Everywhere in the world... there is some kind of greeting. But here (in the United States) the kids aren't greeting the parents and the parents are allowing it. They are tiptoeing around their children."

Families are in flux. Their lives together are cluttered.

Little moments. Lots of them. Lost.

Wealth and fame and Millennials

A study by the Pew Research Center documents that First-Wave Millennials rate their top two priorities in life as becoming rich and famous.

In this 2006 survey, with a ± 5 percent margin of error, 81 percent of then eighteen- to twenty-five-year-olds said getting *rich* is their generation's #1 or #2 priority, while being *famous* is the other goal.

In a *USA Today* story about these generational values, consumer psychologist Kit Yarrow of San Francisco's Golden Gate University worries that Millennials are in for "a sense of emptiness and depression" as they "put their validation and self-worth into what people who aren't close to them think of them."

Big picture

But, big picture, Millennials and their parents seem to like that they are a more nurtured generation than Xers. And Millennials feel like a generation, much like the G.I.s and Boomers do, because they know their age cohort shares very unique formative years' times and teachings.

In other words, they're aware that, from coast to coast, people their age have a common core, a "shared center."

Do not call us Gen Y

Millennials make one request: *don't call us Generation Y and don't call us Echo Boomers,* as some marketers and some media are doing.

To them, Gen Y sounds like their generation is nothing more than a continuation of Generation X. And they'll tell you, *We're not them. We're different from Gen X.* And they're right. ABC News conducted a poll about this as leading-edge Millennials were entering adulthood, and before this generation had been named, and Millennials – *not* Generation Y – was their top choice. Got that, news media?

U.S. Army recruitment campaign

In the early 2000s, the U.S. Army created a new advertising tagline for its recruitment campaign.

"An Army of One."

That tagline – *An Army of One* – is excellent Gen X messaging. Xers are self-reliant, independent, individualistic. Xers are 59,000,000 armies of one.

But then, America went to war soon after the September 11th attack. And the Army then needed to recruit both me-generation Xers and we-generation, team-play Millennials, who are growing up more patriotic and more nationalistic in their thinking than Xers did.

In one TV commercial, the Army does a nice job of creating two-generation appeal:

As we view visual images that constantly switch from *individual* soldiers (Gen X appeal) to *groups* of soldiers (Millennial appeal), here's part of the voiceover:

"An American soldier serves more than his army. He is a selfless defender of our rights and our freedoms." (This is good messaging to the September 11th, patriotic Millennials.) "He is proof that one soldier can and does make a difference." (Good messaging to self-reliant, individualistic Xers.)

So with this single TV spot... *multigenerational* messaging.

Extended adolescence
College debt
Credit card debt
Uncertain job market
What's the hurry?
Hooking up

A significant revolution is underway. It has a label: "Extended Adolescence."

Twenty-something Millennials and Xers are living at home with Mom and Dad in significant numbers in this country, and they're probably permanently redefining what it's like to live life in one's twenties, for four primary reasons:

- College debt.
- Credit card debt.

- Uncertain job and paycheck security for young adults.
- And, Millennials know they're probably going to live well beyond 100, which means they're going to work until they're eighty or ninety or one hundred or longer, so *what's the hurry!?*

And with Mom and Dad paying rent, utilities, and food bills, a good number of twenty-somethings holding down steady jobs have significant discretionary income, and a lot of marketers of higher-end products and services – pricey jewelry, alcohol, apparel, and others – are now advertising to this Extended Adolescence in pursuit of that discretionary money.

Millennials are using their first decade of adulthood to *sample* jobs and careers and employers, have some fun, and remain single before beginning their long-long-long term career commitment and family track. In 2007, the average age for an American woman's first marriage was twenty-seven. In 1970, it was twenty.

Regarding dating and sex, and in harmony with their postponement of serious commitment, Millennials have popularized "hook-ups." Usually, it means casual dating and perhaps oral rather than vaginal sex, with the understanding there are no emotional obligations or expectations. Child experts wonder – and worry – about the long-term consequences of this experience.

Pro-labor?
Pro-union?
Anti-CEO?

We won't know this for certain for a few years, but some of us who study generational dynamics for a living see the Millennials becoming a pro-labor and pro-union generation, and perhaps with an anti-executive attitude.

Why? Millennials' formative years have occurred during the era of the *very rich celebrity CEO*, so this generation has come of age regularly hearing and reading the countless stories of public-company executives receiving unprecedented compensation packages and massive bonuses because those executives pleased Wall Street and shareholders, often by cutting costs by shutting down factories and laying off thousands of American production workers who just happen to be the Millennials' moms and dads.

In this era of the rich getting extremely richer, the middle class taking a pounding, and the average production worker struggling to survive, a generation of American kids has come of age and molded lifelong core values.

And when you layer that perception of *executive excess* over the epidemic of *executive corruption* in this country from the 1980s to the 2000s, it's not difficult to understand a generation that is going to be pro-worker and anti-executive.

And a national award-winning radio spot, a public service announcement that targets Millennials, captures – and reinforces – this generational core value.

The sixty-second spot is actually an anti-smoking message. It was part of the anti-smoking campaign in the state of Minnesota. But it's easy to hear how it also solidifies that growing anti-executive, anti-CEO Millennial Generation core value.

The creative concept for this radio spot begins with a traditional "man-on-the-street interview" — except it's women on the street.

A young adult female interviewer walks up to a couple of Millennial teenage girls standing on the sidewalk, as we hear the noise of cars passing by them out on the street. Here's the dialogue:

Female interviewer: "Alright, you mind answering some questions for me?"
Teenage girl: "No, not at all."
"Alright. For 25.4 million dollars, would you go to school naked for one day?"
"Oh, yeah. Yeah, definitely" (teen girl's sidekick giggles in the background).
"Would you eat road kill for 25.4 million?"
"I think so, yeah" (more sidekick laughter).
"Would you end every single sentence with 'That was a stupid thing to say' for 25.4 million dollars?"
"Yeah, I could do that. That'd work."
"Here's your final question: for 25.4 million dollars, would you hook 3,000 kids a day on something you know will eventually kill a third of them?"
"Never."
"Well, the CEO of the tobacco company that makes Marlboro cigarettes doesn't have a problem with it. Last year, he made 25.4 million dollars in salary with stock options."
"That sucks."
(Voiceover tag): "Corporate tobacco won't tell you the

truth, so we will...."

A radio public service announcement. Anti-smoking? Or, anti-smoking *and* anti-executive?

First-Wave Millennials: Their Future

Well, First-Wave Millennials, here ya come! Pouring into adulthood. And, like all previous generations, you're arriving with your generation's unique core values, which were molded during your unique formative years.

Here's what we don't yet know about your generation:

It appears you're very much like the G.I. and Boomer generations: empowered, engaged, wanting to make a positive difference and just sassy enough to think you *can*, thinking much bigger than just "yourself." But is this true? Or, have older Americans misread your formative years, perhaps because they're hoping too strongly that it is true?

You came of age surrounded by relentless competition from the fellow members of your massive generation in the classroom, on the playing fields, and in just about every other element of your lives. In adulthood, will you carry that same competitive fire into your careers and give America another golden era of innovation and productivity? Or not? People your age in emerging countries are *hungry* in their careers and have their sights set on surpassing America. How hungry are you in your careers? We don't yet know.

Like Xers, your formative years bombarded you with a lot of ethical and moral failures by your nation's leaders in business and government and religion and media. Do you accept this as *the way it is* and plan to behave the same way? Or do you envision an America without these shortcomings and ask, *why not?*

Not to worry. All that's at stake with your answers to these questions is the future of the United States of America.

Chapter 12

Marketing To First-Wave "Mils"
Tips, tactics, and guidelines

REMEMBER:

The information in this book about Millennials applies only to First-Wave'ers, born from 1982 to 1990.

Generational strategy is not reliable with kids generally under age seventeen. They're still forming the generational values they'll keep for life. So for the younger ages, rely instead on age-specific research and strategy. Don't ask yourself, "How do we market to twelve-year-old *Millennials*?" Instead, ask, "How do we market to twelve-year-olds?"

Now, back to our First-Wave Millennials:

This generation is all about technology, all about communications. Cell phones, text messaging, e-mailing, social networking, blogs, and so on.

They are a "we" generation, not a "me" generation like Xers. The technology of their formative years has constantly connected Millennials to other *people*. When Xers were kids, the media du jour tended to *isolate* them from other people.

Millennials like to do things in groups.

As a marketer, you won't be able to command this generation's undivided attention. They are constantly multitasking. TV is important to them, but it's just one instrument in an orchestra of media constantly playing to them.

Millennials care less about brands than Xers do. They believe they *make* retail brands by discovering them. Thus, make your brand discoverable. Don't force-feed it to them with heavy-handed "buy this" messaging.

Millennials are ethnically diverse: about one-third are minorities. Millennials are tolerant of divorced households and gay lifestyles, but traditional values and parental approval are still very important to them.

Millennials *feel* like a generation. Like Boomers and the G.I. Generation, they have major historic events – September 11, the Iraq War, tsunami, Hurricane Katrina – and other shared formative years' experiences that are giving their eighty million members a sense of a common core.

Because they discussed these events so heavily in their classrooms, 9/11 and Katrina and the war have molded a long list of lifelong core values in Millennials: a sense of nation; giving; patriotism; an appreciation of true heroism; team play; selflessness; social activism; a sense that there's more to this world than just "me"; an interest in their own faith and spirituality; and, other core values molded during their generation's unique formative years.

They are the first generation to come of age walking through metal detectors as they arrive at school. When combined with 9/11 and Katrina, one can appreciate their heightened respect for the fragility of their own physical safety.

They feel intense grade and time pressure, because of the constant proficiency testing in school and the competition with their fellow Millennials to gain admittance to their colleges of choice and to land the better jobs. They schedule everything.

This generation possesses a strong sense of community service, in part because schools began to emphasize it during their formative years, and partly because community service in high school looks good on a college or job application.

They are a nurtured generation. Their Helicopter Parents convinced them they are the center of the universe. And they're a heavily adult-supervised generation. They grew up in a more structured environment than Xers. The concern: child experts feel they're growing up "soft" and might not be developing the independence they'll need in the challenging adult world they're now entering.

Their parents' advice and opinions matter to Millennials.

Want to sell to Millennials? Sell it to Mom and Dad too. A U.S. Army recruitment campaign does this, messaging directly to the parents.

As they enter adulthood, employers nationwide consistently describe Millennials' career expectations as "unrealistic," with a flawed sense of entitlement, because they came of age sheltered and given so much time, attention, and materialism by their parents. In their formative years, when Millennial kids were competing in any endeavor, *everybody* got a trophy.

They take multiculturalism for granted. They take globalism for granted.

Like Boomers, they're a massive generation and thus will go through their entire lives amid fierce competition from their fellow Millennials for the best grades, jobs, and promotions. Xers, like the Silents, so few in number, will never have faced the same relentless competition from their own members.

And, Millennials are hearing – or sensing – the same "you're a special generation that has come along at a special time" message that Boomers heard. Millennials are growing up with great expectations for their own generation.

TIPS, TACTICS, GUIDELINES – MARKETING TO MILLENNIALS

"Hip" is mandatory.

Where they go, you go. The mall, the social network,

the cell.

Peer-to-peer recommendations and approval are important. Win over their friends. Some examples:

- Avon created a program whereby girls sixteen to twenty-four would sell its new girls' cosmetic line, "mark."
- P&G launched *Tremor*, which e-mails info on new products to 200,000 teen "connectors," or influencers, who will spread the word about the new product to peers.

Millennials, more plugged in to "the news" than Xers, are reading newspapers and print publications. So, consider exploiting that enthusiasm. Don't assume your message must involve video. College newspapers, with Millennials now dominating the nation's campuses, are *thriving*.

Multimedia messages are probably essential: to find Millennials and to reinforce your message with them.

Various research studies show that high percentages of Millennials value companies and products that support good causes and would be likely to switch brands to one associated with a good cause. Companies that support worthy causes will win Millennial dollars.

Tech and gaming. These are fast-changing categories. Seek the absolute latest research on Millennials' use of, and preferences for, technology and gaming. For example, in the late 2000s, a growing backlash is underway by Millennial college women against college men who "game" for hours every day. The attitude amongst these achieving women is, *if you're squandering that much time on gaming, you don't deserve me.*

Grandparents. Yes, you can use Boomer and Silent Generation grandparents, and their values, to reach the Millennial Generation. Grandparents want to be – and in many instances are – a regular presence in the lives of their Millennial grandchildren. More grandparents than ever are involved in the *primary* care of their grandkids. And overwhelmingly, Millennial grandchildren enjoy their grandparents.

Multigenerational marketing. Millennials generally have a very positive view of older people. They look up to them and welcome their wisdom. Multigenerational marketing and advertising should work well with this generation.

Gender benders. This is a gender-bending generation. The males will pursue traditionally female activities and careers, and females will pursue what was traditionally male.

Viral marketing – "buzz" marketing – is huge with the Millennials.

Millennials are confident, even a little cocky. (Ring a bell, Boomers?) Don't talk down to them.

Time is a luxury many Millennials don't possess. They'll pay for convenience and time saving.

Logo. Millennials are growing up with logos and brands everywhere: stadium names; school soft drink licensing rights; apparel; Web sites; etc. But with their parents, this generation might be bringing logo excess to a halt, or at least slowing it down. Protective parents are aggressively shielding their children from logo commercialism. And *The New York Times*, in a 2004 story about rapidly expanding American Apparel retail T-shirt chain that targets Millennials, wrote the following about the chain's line of apparel: "Perhaps most important to younger consumers who have grown suspicious of corporate branding, there is not a logo in sight." Adds Alex Wipperfurth of marketing firm Plan B in San Francisco, "People are sick of being walking advertisements for clothing. By stripping brands of logos... you are saying you are more about quality than image."

Faith and religion. Take into account Millennials' strong interest in spirituality. But a recent study also documents that Millennials' grasp of traditional religion is *remarkably superficial.* So they're not experts.

They are a generation. It's okay to couch your message in generational terms. Unlike Gen X, Millennials feel like a generation, are developing generational pride, feel special, and if you celebrate them and talk to them as "Millennials," they'll get it. But...

Don't call them Gen Y!! Or Echo Boomers!! Truly, these are deal breakers. Newspapers and magazines use Gen Y, often because the word is shorter than *Millennials* and fits into headlines more easily. Note to print media: this is probably alienating, probably a *big mistake.* Instead, use "Mils".

Chapter 13

First-Wave Mils In The Workplace
Tips, tactics, and guidelines

They came of age coddled, protected, competitive, pressured, adult supervised, idealistic, team oriented, technology dominated, obsessed with fame and celebrity, and with instant access to information and other people.

Remember, they're redefining what it's like to live life in one's twenties: often living with their parents; sampling employers and professions and careers; having some fun; postponing serious commitment.

The lack of career commitment has become a serious dilemma in many industries, especially those whose employers hire twenty-somethings and instantly invest thousands of dollars to train them, only to lose them six weeks later as they "try something else."

For law firms, CPA firms, and other professional-services categories hit hard by this train-'em-then-lose-'em merry-go-round: might you need to begin shifting your target recruiting age from the early or mid-twenties to the late twenties or early thirties? *Twenty-something* in America is undergoing profound and probably permanent change. It's a prodigious shift and serious issue.

From their unique formative years... what do Millennials bring to work?

- Disciplined – they're especially good at hitting deadlines.*
- Comfortable with elders.
- Comfortable in a team/group/collaboration environment.
- But their reliance on the "team" might diminish the independent thinking and risk-taking attributes needed for future leadership.
- Teach them etiquette and workplace ethics.**

* They're the generation of school kids who came of age with constant testing. So they're not intimidated or caught off guard by deadlines. This is a special Millennial strength.

** According to a 2006 study by the Society for Human Resources Management, 75 percent of executives and HR professionals surveyed feel that college graduates possessed minimal skills in terms of professional etiquette and workplace ethics.

- If there's one thing they hunger for more then money, it's responsibility.
- Most productive when presented with clear goals and structure and focus. Without such structure and fo-

cus provided by their bosses, and in sharp contrast to GenX, some Millennials might struggle.

- Optimistic.
- Doing the job well and efficiently is important to them.
- Competitive career'ists, it appears. Like Boomers, Millennials are achievement oriented.
- But they also seek work-life balance. In the job interview, they'll ask, "How much time off do I get?"*
- Seek job security.
- Stable, old-line companies appeal to them, especially when employers make clear the financial rewards and career path.
- Prefer a diverse workforce.
- Will they be especially good leaders, or especially bad ones?**
- Like Xers, they're using early adulthood to sample professions, employers, and cities in which to live.

* Government jobs often have a Millennial-friendly career package of reasonable hours, good benefits, stability and security, and that sense of societal contribution that is important to Millennials. Note to government recruiters: your job postings are often difficult to find and your application process is frequently so complex it's irritating. You're facing a golden opportunity with the Millennial Generation. Don't blow it with bureaucracy and gobbledygook. *Simplify the process.*

** The argument *for* "good leaders": they're group focused, hard working, bold, and visionary. The argument *against*: might not be good at thinking on their feet; possess unrealistic career expectations and sense of entitlement; and, their strong groupthink mentality might render them less adept as stand-alone leaders.

- Seek relevance, sense of purpose and meaning in their work.
- Seek meaningful work at once, often unrealistically.
- Might be impatient to make an impact.
- Want in on creative decisions.
- Unrealistic expectations?*
- Strong sense of entitlement.*
- Crave variety and change.

* My clients repeat it incessantly: "These young people have been so hosed down with praise in childhood that they're beginning their career years with flawed expectations about entry level work." That's why you'll see, below, the suggestion that Millennial new hires probably will need a strong orientation program that, among other things, gets their feet – and heads – on the ground.

Recruiting Millennials

- They're tough to find in this new-media, multimedia era. Find out how and where to reach them (it changes daily) and get creative with your message.*
- Millennial recruits can smell spam from miles away. Make your communications, regardless the medium you use, customized, relevant, and sincere. By the way, this applies to all generations.
- Internships are especially effective recruiting methods. You can identify top prospects and begin to build their loyalty to your organization.

- Stress your organization's stability. "Stability" is looking pretty good to this generation.
- Be diversity friendly.

* Use new media to tell your organization's story and build its brand with Millennial prospects. A *Business Week* magazine story explains how Accenture advertises on coffee cup sleeves on college campuses; Google recruits engineering students to serve pizza to their classmates during exams; JPMorgan Investment Bank runs an interactive derivatives trading game to identify promising candidates.

- Demonstrate your commitment to the individual. Personalize your communications during the recruitment process.
- Stress your organization's civic involvement.
- Can you give them opportunities to work for causes they support?*
- A competitive vacation policy will help you to lure this generation.**

* Philip Morris USA – a *tobacco* company and *cigarette* maker; the devil! – includes in its recruiting message the opportunity for this socially concerned generation to try to develop new technologies that will diminish the harmful effects of cigarettes.

** One banking-industry employer offers three vacation weeks, ten paid holidays, and the option for employees to purchase an additional week of leave.

Managing Millennials

- Strong orientation to ensure a good start. Confront and correct any unrealistic expectations.
- Fast assimilation into the process; don't give them such a slow start they get restless.*
- Can you give entry-level Millennials lots of opportunities to learn early and often?
- Teach realistic expectations.**
- Soft? Might need "protection" in confrontational situations.
- Train them – especially management and leadership candidates – in Generational Workforce Diversity.
- Can you offer tuition reimbursement for outside training?
- Reward them with more responsibility as fast as you reasonably can. This engenders their loyalty.
- Give structure and clear rules.***

* But at the same time, explain to them how entry-level tasks – which they might consider tedious and unimportant – are important to the organization and to their future.

** Because of Millennials' frequent unrealistic expectations as they enter their work years, a senior executive at one of my seminars described them as "space cadets!" So I advise my clients to begin a new hire orientation program with two sentences. Sentence number one: *Millennials, THIS... is Planet Earth.* Sentence number two: *If you want to become CEO of our international conglomerate, you need to understand that it might take you twenty, twenty-five, maybe even thirty days."*

*** Millennials came of age in a more structured, adult-supervised environment than prior generations. As they enter their career years, that structure – that constant guidance from educators, coaches, advisors, and parents – departs. Remember, the older Xers began their work years independent, self-reliant, tough. So if you're training Millennial new hires the same way you trained Xer recruits the prior twenty years, you're preparing for the last war.

- Offer variety: can you give them new opportunities early, and often?*
- Give constant – or at least frequent – feedback and good mentoring. Build solid professional relationships with them. At many organizations, mentoring should not be merely a "program," but instead a "culture."
- About mentoring: don't simply give them more work. Listen. Help them to develop a career path.
- Enable two-way feedback: ask-me-anything chats/lunches with senior management.
- Use their "we" approach.
- Personalize their work.
- Establish clear rules on technology. May your employees use their fifteen-minute breaks to instant-message or shop online? How about the use of iPods? What is appropriate, and when?
- Exploit technology in recruiting and managing them.**

* Key Bank offers a rotational program during new employees' first year on the job, training them in various departments to help those who aren't certain as to what they want to do.

** They're the Technology Generation, accustomed to getting information in short capsules, not lengthy explanations. Some employers are now using computer games and simulations to recruit and train Millennials.

- Establish unambiguous dress and appearance codes, if necessary.
- Create a culture and an infrastructure that enables collaboration.
- Can you design long-term career development plans for, and with, them?
- A competitive salary isn't *everything* to this generation, especially at entry level. So to retain them, create psychological and emotional bonds to your organization.
- Because of the shorthand of instant messaging, their use of the language – semantics, syntax, punctuation – might be significantly inaccurate. If this is a potential detriment to the organization, train them.
- For larger companies with geographically-scattered employees, online video will become a growing, Millennial-prompted, and ultimately less expensive method of communicating with all employees.

THE FINAL THOUGHT

None of us was able to choose the year we were born.

So none of us was able to choose which two decades in time would become our formative years and *shape us for life.*

So none of us was able to choose the generation to which we belong.

When we all acknowledge these three realities, we begin to make peace with the *other* generations.

And with our own.

That's when the generation gaps begin to shrink.

And it's when we find ourselves beginning to truly *root* for those other generations to find their own unique happiness, security, and success in life. And we hope they'll root for our generation, too.

When that occurs, we then focus upon the values we American generations have in *common*, instead of the ones we don't.

In her classic *Beautiful People*, singer/songwriter Melanie Safka expresses the hope - and the exciting *promise* - of intergenerational understanding:

Beautiful people...
You ride the same subway as I do
Every morning.
That's got to tell you something.
We've got so much in common:
I go the same direction that you do.

So if you take care of me...
Well, then...
I'll take care of you.
'Cause all of the beautiful people do....

ABOUT THE AUTHOR

Chuck Underwood is the founder/principal of The Generational Imperative, Inc., a generational consultancy based in Cincinnati. He consults corporations and organizations nationwide on Generational Marketplace Strategy and Generational Workforce Strategy.

He began his study of generational dynamics in the mid-'80s, long before the discipline came to the widespread attention of American business. He is a pioneering scholar in this field.

Formally trained in qualitative research methodology and focus group moderating at the Burke Institute, he conducts proprietary research for his clients and his own firm.

He spent his earlier career as an award-winning broadcast journalist and creator and producer of original (and, again, award-winning) television programming.

His media career and generational study merged in the early 2000s, when he produced a television talk show special about the generations. Soon after the show aired, he was asked to present Generational Marketing Strategy to the prestigious National Summit on Retirement Savings in Washington, D.C.

Serendipity: American business was now ready to learn about generational dynamics, and Chuck Underwood was ready to explain it.

He has taken his rightful place as a preeminent authority on generational study. Consulting, speaking, and conducting generational research throughout the United States and Canada, Chuck also authors magazine and newspaper columns, guest lectures at universities, and is regularly consulted by reporters for their generational news stories for network television, national magazines, trade publications, radio, and the nation's major newspapers.

His company's Web site is:
www.genimperative.com

You're welcome to e-mail Chuck at:
info@genimperative.com

921177

Made in the USA